Living *and* Thriving *in the* Parent-Teen Relationship

STEPHANIE ILES
and ANGELE SUAREZ

Copyright © 2023 Stephanie Iles and Angele Suarez
All rights reserved
First Edition

Fulton Books
Meadville, PA

Published by Fulton Books 2023

ISBN 979-8-88731-397-9 (paperback)
ISBN 979-8-88731-398-6 (digital)

Printed in the United States of America

To our wonderful husbands, for all their love and support.

Contents

Acknowledgements

We both want to thank Fulton Publishing for accepting our manuscript and helping us make this a reality. This is all so new to us, and hope that by the time this is in print, we will have learned so much from you.

From Steph:

My biggest shoutout goes to my coauthor, Angele. You helped me become the author I always wanted to be. I have dreamed of writing a book and becoming an author since I was eight years old. Who knew I would make a better coauthor? I love you, dear friend. To many more books together.

Thank you to my husband, David, who has supported me in so many ways in this process, the biggest being his encouragement. Thank you to my boys, Nick and Jared, who were the reason I wanted to become a better parent. I love watching you both now as adults. A special thank you to my daughter-in-law, Sawyer, who was kind enough to read a rough draft of the book and offer feedback (even though she just had a baby). Love to my mom, brother, and grandkids.

I would like to thank all the professors I had at Western Seminary and my fellow students for making learning such an amazing journey. I am thankful for them teaching me how to integrate my faith with my work as an MFT. I am also thankful to all my clients over the years and look forward to clocking many more clinical hours in the future doing what I love.

From Angele:

Thank you to my coauthor, Stephanie, who helped me to take a million book ideas and begin by just writing one (for now). Thank you for your love of writing and collaboration to make this a reality. I love you, my forever friend and coauthor.

I would like to thank the many teenagers and families (you know who you are) who have allowed me to share in your journeys and lives of recovery. Thank you for your trust; it is always an honor for me to be invited into your lives.

To my husband, Ron, and four amazing stepchildren, Maya, Alexa, Caressa, and Brando. This family has changed my life forever because they gave me the opportunity to know what it means to love unconditionally by choice and not just by blood. You are forever my family.

Chapter 1

INTRODUCTION

Where did my little kid go? It's amazing how different the teen years are from those early years of toddlers and elementary school shenanigans. It can be difficult to transition from parenting a ten-year-old to parenting a fourteen-year-old. You watch your children move away from little sticky hands exploring everything, hearing "Why?" a million times, and adoring eyes looking at you with admiration to big stinky shoes left everywhere, hearing "Why not?" a million times, and then looking at you like you are clueless. It's not all negative. In fact, it can be one of the most rewarding times as a parent.

It's a time for them to explore their identity, become independent, learn to think critically, and explore their future. If you have developed a good relationship, then this is a time in which you can laugh together, talk about religion and politics, be philosophical about life and death, and share hobbies and ideas. They are on the cusp of being part of your club known as adulthood. Our families had movie nights, game nights, and camping trips. We played music together, we attended events as a family, we sat around talking about the world, and we did "unplug days" (where we turned off electronics and found adventure in "the real world"). We want that kind of experience for you.

It's hard. Not all parents have the tools they need to manage teen problems. No parent was expecting COVID-19 and a quarantine to hit, for example. Who knew teaching at home and hours of online schooling were going to be something you would all have to maneuver? The rise in anxiety, depression, and online addiction was devastating during this time. Families had stress and tension in their lives like never before. The pandemic seemed to highlight family struggles.

The teen years are built upon the early years. Some things you may have control over, and others you don't. You wake up one day, and you have a kid in middle school. Things start to change. They might start using a tone in their voice that they don't even hear. They might feel feelings they have never felt before and react to those feelings as though it's your fault they are feeling them. They push you away one day and need a hug the next. They start experimenting with their clothes, their hair, their music—well, everything really.

The teen years are sometimes painful (for both parent and teen), but they can also be amazing. This is a time when parenting still matters a tremendous amount, but you can't use little kid parenting tactics on teens. Parenting is difficult, whether you're parenting a toddler or a teen. It takes work, determination, and resilience on the part of the parent. There will be key times when you will have to put in extra work but other times when you will get to just enjoy your kids' company.

This book is designed to be a guide to help you navigate many of the challenges you now face in parenting a teen. You are not alone. This is going to be challenging, but with the right tools, community support, and a good discipline plan, you will find it very rewarding. We hope this book will help you not only to better navigate parenting during the teen years but also to thrive in your relationship with your teen as they become young adults. We think it's worth it.

So Where to Begin?
The Excitement and Grief of Change

A big part of helping your teen will be to grieve their transition. It is not about being sad that they are growing up; it is more the process of saying goodbye to their "little self" and starting on their new adventure, toward adulthood, with them. With any change in life, there is a grieving process. Some people struggle with the idea of being happy and sad at the same time. It is sad your child isn't little anymore, but it is also exciting that they are becoming more independent and growing into who they are going to be. Trying to control or stop the transition process will only make parenting more difficult. The goal is to maintain your parent-child relationship while letting go of expectations.

Try This
Grieving Transition

Make a memory book or box. Wrap up their childhood by creating a memento of those years. Find pictures and trinkets that remind you of the highlights of those years. Create something special that will allow you to say goodbye to the old and embrace the new part of your journey. This grieving process is not for them, but for you, the primary caregiver. Allow yourself to cry if need be. Be intentional about letting yourself feel the change that is happening.

There are some major role changes during this time. Your expectations will need to shift, because in middle school, kids start to see their friends as the most important people in their lives. Parents become second-class citizens. It can feel like you just went from "hero" to "zero" if you are holding tightly to the expectation that you will have the same kind of relationship. It's hard for parents because a lot of parents have spent years putting their kids first. It can feel like four to seven years of rejection. The somewhat weird part is that they need you. It just looks different.

Your kids will also start listening to other adults and asking for their advice (a favorite teacher, social media influencers, authors or musicians, youth pastors, or other mentors). This shift can be very drastic and sometimes painful for the parents. Imagine you tell your kids a hundred times how important college will be, for example, and they only seem to ignore you. Then one day, they come bursting in from school, and they tell you all about how they decided to go to college—not because you said so, but because their teacher told them it was a good idea or their friend is going, and they say it's really cool. Your teen talks about it as though you have never mentioned it. You might feel like it's personal. It's not.

When parents start taking this "rejection" personally, people get hurt. It can be especially hard for parents who have poured everything into their children and, maybe, neglected their marriage or even themselves. All parents will do a certain amount of grieving as their kids go through this process. If you have not found balance in your life and your kids are the most important things to you, this will be an especially hard time. Grieving this transition will become critical.

Recognizing Healthy Relationships

Building your own community at this time can be a game changer. Having your own friends to talk with and spend time with will help you feel supported and loved. If you let your marriage fall to the back burner, it's time to rekindle the flame. If you are a single parent, then maybe spending time with friends learning new activities can be a good form of self-care. Doing something for yourself might feel selfish, but it is the exact opposite. Self-care will help you to avoid the true selfish move of making your teen your friend.

> ## TRY THIS
> ## DEVELOPING YOUR OWN COMMUNITY
>
> PEOPLE THRIVE WHEN THEY HAVE ONE TO THREE REALLY CLOSE FRIENDS. THESE ARE THE FRIENDS WHO LISTEN TO YOU WHEN THINGS GET TOUGH, AND YOU DO THE SAME FOR THEM. MAKE A LIST OF FRIENDS AND PEOPLE WHO SUPPORT YOU (YOUR KIDS SHOULD NOT BE ON THIS LIST). HIGHLIGHT YOUR TOP THREE. MAKE SURE TO MAKE INTENTIONAL CHOICES TO REACH OUT TO THEM REGULARLY AND INCLUDE THEM IN YOUR LIFE. MAKE PLANS TO HAVE DINNER, GO FOR A WALK, TALK ON THE PHONE, ETC.

Parents can have a close relationship with their teens without being their friend. It means being consistent and having solid boundaries. What might look like rejection is their process of becoming healthy, functioning adults. It's their individuation process. You are there to support your kids; they are not here to support you. If you have a good connection based on respect and trust, they will have your values as they explore the world, and they will most likely share their experience with you. When they are full-grown adults caring for themselves, then they can connect with you on a peer level.

The role of the parent is very important during these years, it's not easy, and it is rarely glamorous. Even though your teen is pushing you away, you being there and being a consistent part of their life will allow for stability and safety from early childhood all the way through to young adulthood. If you provide this for your teen, you may find they come back to you looking for friendship when they are adults.

It is never too late to have an impact on your kids' lives. How much and in what way you impact them will be based on your approach. Being "the boss" can cause conflict and real rejection from both parent and child. Demanding that your teen practice your values and morals can be a losing battle. If you approach your teen with two-way respect, allow for natural consequences, and use creative discipline, your odds of maintaining a healthy relationship just increased. The kind of relationship you are building is important. It can be fun, exciting, and entertaining, but sometimes you will have to speak difficult truths into their lives.

I (Stephanie) used to joke with my boys about the movie *Psycho.* The main character, Norman Bates, says, "A boy's best friend is his mother" (Hitchcock, 1960), and I would make a crazy face at my boys. My friends were my friends, and my boys had their friends. Did it take away from hanging out, playing games, going on vacations, or eating dinners together? No! I loved spending time with my boys during the teen years, but they were not my "friends." They had a more honorable job of being my sons. Give your teen the same honor.

Modeling Caution; Celebrating Passion

If you demand respect and have only a one-way authoritarian relationship with your teens, you will not get very far. You can demand respect and communication, but it will not get you the results you want. Parenting is about modeling the behaviors you would like to see your kids engage in. If you are *demanding* that your teen clean their room, be prepared for your teen to *demand* that you leave them alone. Instead, setting up expectations about chores and behavior and having clear consequences (both positive and negative) is more respectful than *demanding* something. There will be times when you will have to be firm in your boundaries and consistent with your rules; this should still be done with respect and communication.

One of the biggest jobs a parent has is to model humility and accountability. Here's the thing: everyone makes mistakes and poor choices. It is very important to model for your teen how to acknowledge your errors, talk about your mistakes, and learn from them. Teens can gain a lot from a parent who says, "Listen, I was wrong. I should not have talked to you in such a disrespectful way. I will do my best to be aware of when I am feeling frustrated, and I will take a break until I am able to continue the conversation." This teaches your teen resiliency and how to be accountable for their own mistakes. You would be modeling humility, flexibility, and a growth mindset (Dweck, 2006).

The part of the teen brain that deals with big emotions and impulsive behavior develops a lot faster than the part of the brain that regulates emotions and thoughtful decision-making (Berger, 2008, p. 375). As a parent, you might find yourself asking, "Why did they do that? Didn't they think it through?" The part of your brain that makes you "boring" is the part that is still developing for them. Well-thought-out decisions are an adult trait. Be patient. Model the skill of thinking it through. Even better, model how to fix a bad decision like an adult, with accountability, responsibility, and restitution.

There is a beautiful side to being impulsive and passionate. Teens have big ideas, and they can often be overwhelmed by them, but inspire them to take big actions. We did a search online for teen philanthropists and got article after article of things teens have done to change the world. A wonderful example of this is Zack Hunter of Loose Change to Loosen Chains. This kid heard slavery still existed in the world when he was studying American history in the seventh grade (End Slavery Now, 2014). He overcame his public speaking fears and boldly began raising thousands of dollars, which he donated to end slavery worldwide. Teens are capable of amazing and wonderful things given the right kind of inspiration.

Remember, if you are surprised by all the changes they are going through, imagine how they feel. They have emotions they have never had before and might not even know how to label them. They feel chaotic in a chaotic world. If their family life has also been chaotic, then they may not know how to behave in any other manner than with chaos. It's not too late to bring balance to their lives.

> ## TRY THIS
> ## VALUES DEVELOPMENT
>
> EVERYONE IN THE FAMILY LISTS THEIR TOP FIVE VALUES. LIST AN ACTION YOU TOOK RECENTLY DEMONSTRATING THIS VALUE. SHARE YOUR LIST WITH EACH OTHER. LOOK AT THE WEEK AHEAD, AND THINK OF ONE ACTION EACH OF YOU CAN TAKE TO ADVANCE ONE OF YOUR VALUES.
>
> CORE VALUES LIST: AUTHENTICITY, ACHIEVEMENT, ADVENTURE, BALANCE, BOLDNESS, CAREER, COMPASSION, CHALLENGE, COMMUNITY, CONTRIBUTION, CREATIVITY, DETERMINATION, FAIRNESS, FAITH, FAME, FRIENDSHIPS, FUN, GROWTH, HAPPINESS, HONESTY, INFLUENCE, JUSTICE, KINDNESS, KNOWLEDGE, LEADERSHIP, LOVE, MEANINGFUL WORK, PEACE, PLEASURE, RECOGNITION, REPUTATION, RESPECT, RESPONSIBILITY, ROMANCE, SECURITY, SELF-RESPECT, SPIRITUALITY, STABILITY, SUCCESS, STATUS, TRUSTWORTHINESS, WEALTH, AND WISDOM (TO LIST A FEW)

THE DEVELOPMENTAL STAGES

Erik Erikson, one of our role models, is a psychologist who identified developmental stages. He described teens this way, "The adolescent mind is essentially a mind of the moratorium, a psychosocial stage between childhood and adulthood, and between the morality learned by the child, and the ethics to be developed by the adult" (Erikson, Childhood and Society, 1963). His definition basically describes a time of transition. Change, change, change!

In childhood, their role was to learn trust, autonomy, initiative, and industry. That means that they should enter the teen years with a sense of hope in their environment, some basic self-control skills, an ability to create new things, and a curiosity about how things work and where everything belongs (Berger, 2008). When the family system is broken, those things become distorted. This can make the approach to the teen years a little bumpier (although it's usually a bumpy ride, no matter what) because the next stage is identity, and it's a big one; if they aren't prepared through the other stages to go through this, they will have a distorted sense of self.

Developmental stage	Basic virtue	Age range	Environmental influences
Trust vs. mistrust	Hope	0–1½	Primary caregiver
Autonomy vs. shame	Will	1½–3	Core caregivers
Initiative vs. guilt	Purpose	3–5	Parents, family, friends
Industry vs. inferiority	Competency	5–12	Parents, teachers, peers
Identity vs. role confusion	Fidelity	12–18	Peers, significant other
Intimacy vs. isolation	Love	18–40	Partner, friends
Generativity vs. stagnation	Care	40–65	Family, community
Ego Integrity vs. Despair	Wisdom	65+	Everyone

(Berger, 2008) (Erikson, 1963)

THE IDENTITY STAGE

What is the "identity stage," and why is it so important? This is the stage of examining oneself to decide "Who am I going to be?" They spent their childhood being told who they are and mimicking their parents. In middle school, kids are looking around them, watching others (peers and adults), and wondering, "Do I want to be like that person?" They go through the process of "trying things on" for a while and making decisions about their future. It can be stressful. Teens, in every generation, may appear selfish to the adults around them because, in some ways, they are. Their thoughts are on their development.

So what are some of the downsides of your teen not fully exploring this stage in their life? They might experience role confusion and uncertainty. This means that because they are uncertain about who they are and where they fit in, they struggle to form meaningful relationships in their lives. This is often seen with adults who move from job to job and relationship to relationship. They are searching for their place in life through external experiences trying to fill a void, versus knowing themselves and sharing their identity with the outside world.

While processing who they are going to be, they have the conversations of their childhood in the back of their mind, helping with their decisions. With some, it might be "You are unlovable." With others, it could be "You rock, and you got this!" The internal conversation is varied, and while building relationships with your teens, it would be helpful to explore how they view and feel about themselves. It is an opportunity to help them replace their negative thoughts with your supportive voice. Developing good communication habits with your teen will be a cornerstone to having a good relationship with your soon-to-be adult.

Mistakes Equal Learning

Teens experiencing mistakes during the identity stage creates a teaching opportunity for the parent. Mistakes? Yes, we want them to make mistakes. Without mistakes, they are not living their boldest selves. They are missing out on opportunities to take risks and stretch themselves. And it's an opportunity for you to teach them how to recover from falling on their face.

There are two negative ways of viewing mistakes that can negatively impact their development. First, mistakes are bad and should be avoided at all costs. This can create anxiety and overly cautious behavior. Second, mistakes are shameful and should always be punished. This can lead to people hiding and lying about errors, instead of learning and growing from them. They are going to make mistakes—embrace that idea.

Mistakes are a great opportunity. It's a chance to learn resilience and flexibility. What a great lesson to teach your young adult. They make a mistake, and you are there to help them take responsibility, make it right, and get back on track. The process should be a collaboration of ideas and good communication. Yelling and demanding do not support self-awareness and develop skills that will help them in the future. Plus, remember that you are modeling for your teen, so if you yell when you are angry, then your teen will likely yell too (and guess who they are going to be yelling at…yeah…you).

The hardest thing to watch is when your kids make the same mistakes you made. You want to rescue them. The best way to help them with those mistakes is to be honest about your journey. Rather than judging them and making them feel shame, try modeling your own growth. Teens connect with honesty and compassion. Share your story, ask how their experience feels different, and listen without fixing it. Collaborate on how to address mistakes with accountability and follow-through.

> ### TRY THIS
> ### BUILD TRUST
>
> IF YOUR TEEN HAS HAD A DIFFICULT LIFE, THEY MAY STRUGGLE TO TRUST THEMSELVES. YOU MAY NOTICE THEY OFTEN RESPOND WITH "I DON'T CARE" OR "I DON'T KNOW." GIVE THEM LITTLE CHOICES ON A REGULAR BASIS THAT HAVE NO WRONG ANSWERS.
>
> *DO YOU WANT TO WATCH THIS MOVIE OR THAT ONE? DO YOU WANT TEA OR HOT CHOCOLATE? DO YOU WANT TO START YOUR HOMEWORK NOW OR TAKE A QUICK BREAK? DO YOU WANT TO GO TO THIS RESTAURANT OR THAT ONE?*
>
> THESE DECISIONS MAY SEEM SIMPLE, BUT MAKING CHOICES BUILDS TRUST IN ONESELF. THE KEY FOR THE PARENT IS TO NOT CRITICIZE ANY DECISIONS IN THIS EXERCISE. SO CHOOSE YOUR TEEN'S OPTIONS CAREFULLY. IF THEY RESPOND WITH "I DON'T KNOW," THEN SAY, "I'LL GIVE YOU TIME TO THINK ABOUT IT." INTROVERTS TAKE LONGER TO RESPOND.
>
> THIS CAN ALSO BE DONE AS A GAME OF "THIS OR THAT," WHERE YOU ASK BIZARRE QUESTIONS AT DINNER AND EVERYONE HAS TO PICK ONE. (EXAMPLE: WOULD YOU RATHER FLY OR READ MINDS?)

A NEW GENERATION

The teens of past generations and the current teens have a lot in common. They are carving out their own culture and identity. They often have their own language and slang. Their music speaks to them. They are trying to let go of childhood and become adults who can make their own decisions and support themselves. They are mostly focused on themselves, who they are, and how they fit into their community. This is all very normal.

Some things are very different for this newer generation. The digital age has changed some things we can't completely wrap our minds around as a member of a previous generation: children in middle school who go to a plastic surgeon, asking to look like the "photo filtered" version of themselves, and being bullied not by one, two, or five people, but potentially hundreds (sometimes thousands) of people online, some of whom they don't even know. They are surrounded by a constant bombardment of advertising, flashy links, anonymous hate speech, and sometimes an addiction to their cell phones and computers that seems obsessive.

With times being different and a digital world that is constantly changing, it is also important to have compassion for their unique experience with it. They are constantly under pressure from peers, both online and in "real life," who have expectations of communication via text we never had. "You must respond within the hour or less, or we are done being friends." They are globally connected, but they have so little in-person connection. Some of today's teens have friends only online. Don't dismiss their issues just because it doesn't make sense to you.

TRY THIS
GET UNPLUGGED!

TAKE A BREAK AS A FAMILY. PUT ALL TECHNOLOGY AWAY AND DO AN ACTIVITY THAT DOES NOT REQUIRE BEING PLUGGED IN. THE MORE FUN YOU HAVE WITH IT, THE MORE YOU WILL ENTICE YOUR TEENS TO ENGAGE. LEARN A NEW SKILL BY TAKING A CLASS TOGETHER. YOUR TEEN MIGHT GET TO SEE YOU STRUGGLE WITH SOMETHING TOO.

Having a better relationship with your teen is very possible. The biggest pieces of the puzzle are communication and respect. Developing your listening skills, understanding your wants and your teen's needs, having healthy expectations, setting safe boundaries that are consistent, working collaboratively on discipline, and spending quality time are some of the many things that we will help you develop.

We hope that as a family, you will be able to live and thrive in your relationships together and see your teen become the adult they are meant to be. Throughout the book, we will be highlighting aspects of our THRIVE model.

- *Trust*—Building trust means being honest with yourself and your teen. It's being consistent in your reactions and clear with your expectations. It means following through every time.
- *Heal*—To heal your family, you must understand the whole system. It is understanding your struggle, separate and in conjunction, with your teen. It is finding the humility to be weak and imperfect and then accepting the imperfectness of it all. It is being courageous enough to implement change.
- *Respect*—To have respect, it must be mutual. Loving your teen for who they are, speaking honestly, and using a kind tone model the kind of respect you would want from them. Respect can also be defined as respecting yourself and who you are as a parent—knowing your strengths and understanding when you need to ask for help.
- *Invite*—This is the core of collaboration. Invite your teen to participate with you.
- *Validate*—Validating that everyone has their own set of emotions that have value is very impactful for the family system. Honoring those feelings and listening to each other will build relationships and create healthy adults.
- *Enjoy*—Have fun! Enjoy your family. Enjoy your teen.

Chapter 2

PARENTING WITHOUT FEAR

Teens come with many different parts to their personalities. Some are loud, others quiet, some like sports, some like the arts, some enjoy reading or cooking or gardening, some like to be around a lot of people, and some prefer one or two good friends—the list of characteristics is endless. Teens are looking at themselves and listening to the world and wondering, *Where do I fit in? Where do I belong?* Accepting who they are is a big part of the teen years, and their parents are a very crucial part of the process.

Encouragement goes a long way in helping your teen accept themselves. Unfortunately, the world will occasionally use words with negative connotations like obnoxious, nerdy, stubborn, rebellious, lazy, or any word that follows "too," like "too quiet"—again, sadly, the list is long. These negative labels are doing damage to your teen. Every person on this planet has strengths and weaknesses. We believe the goal of parenting a teen is to focus on their strengths and provide opportunities to challenge their weaknesses. Teens already have enough self-doubt about who they are, even if it is disguised as "all about me." A teen's job is to create a sense of self during these years, and fortunately or unfortunately, it will be heavily influenced by what other people think about them. We hope that you develop enough trust with your teen to have a strong influence on them.

Everyone also has a core personality that drives who they are. For every personality type, there are ways to develop positive behaviors given the proper environment. Parents need to remember that some of the behavior they will witness in their teens was modeled by their parents. It's important to consider that communication is affected by your body language and tone. You can guarantee you will have an eye-rolling teen if you have ever done the same. The good news is that most weaknesses can be honed into strengths (that's true of parents as well).

Let me clarify by sharing some examples. People might say being a procrastinator is "wrong" or "bad," but procrastinators have some amazing strengths. They are good under pressure. They can handle last-minute changes better than the planner type. It's important to find opportunities to focus this trait on something productive. Another example is the descriptor "stubborn." Parents might see this as a huge problem. If you change the word to loyal, tenacious, diligent, or unwavering, then it gives you an opportunity to help them make that part of their personality something special.

TRY THIS
BUILDING STRENGTHS OUT OF WEAKNESSES

THIS EXERCISE CAN BE DONE ALONE OR WITH YOUR TEEN. MAKE A LIST OF THE LABELS YOU HAVE BEEN CALLED, GIVEN, OR BELIEVED. CIRCLE THE POSITIVE ONES IN BLUE. FOR THE ONES LEFT OVER, CROSS THEM OUT AND REPLACE THEM WITH A POSITIVE WORD OR STATEMENT. EXAMPLES MIGHT BE:

NEGATIVE	POSSIBLE POSITIVES
STUBBORN	LOYAL, TENACIOUS
OBNOXIOUS	ENERGETIC, ENTERTAINING
TOO QUIET	THOUGHTFUL, GOOD LISTENER
TOO SENSITIVE	EMPATHETIC, SENTIMENTAL
UNLOVABLE	MATCHED WITH THE WRONG PEOPLE
UPTIGHT	ORGANIZED, DETAIL-ORIENTED
FAILURE	RISK-TAKER

YOU GET THE IDEA. NOW THAT YOU HAVE YOUR LIST OF POSITIVES, START DEVELOPING THOSE QUALITIES. PICK ONE THAT YOU CAN WORK ON THIS WEEK BY TAKING AN ACTION THAT IS DIRECTLY LINKED TO LIVING OUT THAT POSITIVE QUALITY.

*YOU CAN ALSO MAKE A LIST FOR YOUR TEEN. WORK ON ENCOURAGING THE POSITIVES. IF YOU HAVE POSITIVE EXPECTATIONS OF YOUR TEEN, THEN IT WILL GUIDE YOUR BEHAVIOR TO DEVELOP THAT PART IN THEM.

Parents sometimes make the mistake of trying to change who their child is rather than accepting who they are and helping them become a better version of themselves. You are not going to turn your "wild" teen into a quiet bookish type. "Taming" your teen through tough discipline will be a long and painful battle and may only result in broken self-esteem in your teen and a tired parent. Instead, help them develop skills to be dynamic, passionate, and creative. A "rule breaker" can learn to use grit to fight injustice, start a company, and be innovative. On the flip side, you are not going to turn your "brooding" teen into a social butterfly. You can't push them into an endless string of social situations, hoping it will take them. There is an opportunity to help them be thoughtful, contemplative, empathetic, and good listeners. We are not suggesting that you stop implementing consequences for poor choices and actions, but we are suggesting that the implementation of these consequences be presented in a manner that your teen will learn, listen, and grow.

The more you push your teen away from the core of who they are, rather than guiding them to a better version of themselves, the more you create anxiety and depression. Acceptance and guidance are the keys to parenting a teen. Your teen hears enough negative feedback from society, social media, and peers. Parents have the opportunity to see their beautiful potential and highlight their strengths.

How do we separate behavior from personality when trying to help a teen improve who they are? Behavior isn't permanent. Skills like leadership, communication, making friends, critical thinking, organization, dependability, and more can all be taught and practiced. So how do you know when it's part of who they are and when it's a skill? Try describing their behavior using a verb—to complain, to forget, to sass. These are the behaviors that can be refined. Any statement that starts with "You are…" is going to be about who they are. This may or may not seem obvious, or maybe it sounds nitpicky, but the distinction can be huge.

Another obvious experience for many parents is repetition. Parents will, at some point, hear themselves say, "How many times do I have to tell you…?" The answer might be "A whole lot!" It's important to remember that a skill takes time, practice, and modeling to learn. None of us could pick up a violin for the first time and crank out some beautiful Mozart pieces. It will more likely sound like an angry cat. Your teen is going to struggle and make mistakes, and so will you. Have compassion, patience, and love for both of you.

Always keep the goal in your sights. It's about having a better relationship with your teens in the long run and guiding them into becoming healthy, independent adults in the future. This takes work, and there will be times when it may seem like they don't like you at all. It might even feel like a slow process. Parenting is not for cowards. But you may have more strengths as a parent than you think.

Parent Strengths

Your first biggest strength as a parent is that you want to help your teen. We know this because you are reading a book on parenting. It is that hope and willingness to do something, which will drive your efforts. You love your teen better than anyone else. Not only should you give yourself permission to make the decisions that best suit your family, but also be okay with making mistakes. Let's look at some other qualities you may have or want to develop during this process.

Be able to ask for help

This is tricky because sometimes, when things are going poorly, there are a lot of people with big opinions and quick advice, and not all of it will fit your teen or family. Books, experts, friends, grandparents, and online forums will all have different advice, and it's important to find what works best for you. Whenever you are in doubt, ask yourself what values you would like to model for your teen. Still the best form of parenting is through what we do and not what we say. Be thoughtful when asking for help. Talk to friends and professionals (pediatricians, family therapists, teachers, and school counselors) who share your values. Ask a lot of questions. Take notes. Make a plan.

TRY THIS
STAY CURRENT

EVERY FEW MONTHS, IT MIGHT BE GOOD TO READ A PAR-
ENTING BOOK, A BOOK THAT YOUR TEEN IS EXCITED ABOUT,
OR SOMETHING ABOUT CURRENT TRENDS (AUDIOBOOKS
ARE FUN TOO). MAYBE SUBSCRIBE TO A PODCAST OR BLOG
THAT KEEPS YOU UP TO DATE WITH WHAT IS POPULAR WITH
TEENS AND WHO THEIR BIGGEST INFLUENCERS ARE.

Building up your community so you have resources can be a big part of good parenting. Be willing to host gatherings so the teens have a safe space to hang out and you will get to know their friends. You can even host events with the whole family, so you can get to know parents who might be going through what you are going through.

Talk to other parents, any parents, even parents who don't know your teen. Finding people who have similar life circumstances can make sharing your struggles easier. Support groups can be a great resource to ask for help. Get to know people of a greater generation who have already successfully navigated parenthood and ask them for guidance.

Be flexible

All people have different personalities, cultural backgrounds, experiences, and perceptions; therefore, your interactions will always be unique to you. We all probably wish there was some giant manual that has, "Day 5940: your teen is going to need help with a breakup today. Do this…" It doesn't exist. All parents are pretty much doing it all by trial and error. So are your teens. Different parenting skills will work for a week, a month, or a year and then feel all wrong suddenly and need some tweaking. Always go back to the basics: respect, communication, and flexibility.

All your kids are going to be different, and being flexible will give you some sanity. When one of your kids is struggling and you feel like all you are doing is getting angry, you may need to think outside the box to create some positive interactions with your teen. When teens say they feel like everyone is "picking on them," it usually means they are starting to feel like they're "the troublemaker" and they may just give in and embrace the role. It is the best time to boost them up and remind them of their strong qualities. Spend some fun time together.

Be willing to learn

Reading a book is a great start. And as we have mentioned already, learning who your teen is is also very important. Listen to them. If they are yelling, it is usually a sign they don't feel heard. Life can get busy, and it's important to slow down and get to know your teen as a young adult. Don't assume who they were at nine years old is still who they are.

It's also important to learn from your own process. Parenting isn't for cowards because it's hard to do. It takes a lot of discipline and growth. You are going to make mistakes, and things are sometimes not going to go as planned. When you make a mistake, don't spend too much time beating yourself up. That's a waste of precious time. Consider what happened. Share it with a fellow parent. Then move on by asking, "What can I do better going forward?" and modeling the ability to recover from a mistake. Show them how you learn from it and then make changes. This skill is very important for your teen.

TRY THIS
LEARNING THROUGH MOVIES

AN EASY WAY TO START A DIALOGUE IS THROUGH MOVIE WATCHING. HAVE A FAMILY MOVIE NIGHT. WATCH THE MOVIES THEY LIKE. ASK QUESTIONS ABOUT WHY THEY LIKE IT. BE CURIOUS. WATCH MOVIES THAT HAVE HIGH SCHOOLERS IN THEM. ASK IF IT'S REALISTIC. ASK WHAT THEY DID GET RIGHT ABOUT HIGH SCHOOL. ASK WHAT THEY GOT WRONG. DON'T MOCK THEIR CHOICE. BE CURIOUS.

I (STEPHANIE) WORKED WITH TEENS FOR YEARS. I WATCHED THE MOVIE *MEAN GIRLS* (WATERS, 2004) BECAUSE THE TEENS I WAS WORKING WITH SAID, "IT'S THE BEST MOVIE EVER." I LEARNED SO MUCH BY WATCHING IT WITH THEM. EVEN WATCHING *THE DARK KNIGHT* (NOLAN, 2008) WITH MY SONS HELPED ME SEE HOW THEY SEE HEROES AND VILLAINS (BRUCE WAYNE MAKES SOME INTERESTING CHOICES).

Be consistent

People learn when they see patterns and make sense of them. If you set up some ground rules for your teen, be clear about the consequences and stick with them. If you don't follow through one day but explode with anger about the same rule the next day, your teen will not learn. Having clear expectations and following through in a consistent manner is the strongest way to develop good habits. Teens have enough change going on in their bodies (hormones, puberty, etc.); they don't need inconsistencies in their family life.

Your actions should match your words. Don't yell at them for being on the computer too long if you are stuck on your phone and ignoring them. If you want them to be the sort of teen who is respectful, forgiving, generous, and kind, then these are the qualities you should consistently be modeling for them. Because teens are in the identity phase, they are judging themselves and their actions, but they might also be watching you.

One of the side effects of teens watching everyone around them with an analytical eye is that they sometimes point out their parents' flaws. It's hard when they point out inconsistencies because it feels disrespectful. Talk about it openly and get back on track to being consistent. It's okay to admit a mistake and apologize. It's also okay to agree to disagree. Your teen will learn from all of it. We know it's hard that you are not the "hero" of their childhood anymore, but it's a great time to teach about being human.

Respect your teens

Yes, they make choices that make no sense to you. Yes, they have moods that come out of nowhere. Yes, they think about themselves a lot. This is what teens are about. Respect that they are still adults in training and are making all kinds of decisions, both healthy and unhealthy. Understand they are not you. They are unique and are trying to figure it out.

When disciplining them, don't yell, but talk to them. Don't have hard or serious conversations in front of their friends and embarrass them. Just because they are in trouble and they are receiving consequences, it doesn't mean you have to be angry with them. At work, if you make a mistake and your boss is yelling at you in front of everyone about what a terrible job you did, how would this impact you? Would you feel embarrassed, angry, or disrespected? Don't do that to your teen. It's a learning process—so teach.

Respect is about treating others the way we want to be treated. Most would struggle to respect someone who doesn't respect them. It's more effective if it's mutual. If you are in a battle with your teen for respect, as a parent, you may need to be the first one to start showing respect. Model for your teen how you want them to treat you. And even when they are not showing you the same respect, keep modeling. It is very difficult to keep yelling at someone who is responding with respect.

Practice good communication

Talk. Talk. Talk. Listen. Listen. Listen. Choose your times to talk wisely. Some teens don't like sitting across from people staring into their faces. Find opportunities to talk shoulder to shoulder. A great example is volunteering to pick your teen and their friends up from events. Yes, this will sometimes mean having to do extra work, but then you can sit and listen in the car. Hear what they say to each other and what they enjoyed about their time together. When their friends are dropped off, you can then chat with your teen as they sit next to you. This is a great opportunity.

If you find yourself being defensive or yelling, then you have stopped communicating effectively. Defensiveness is not productive, nor is it warranted. You are the parent, and you do not need to defend yourself; you only need to communicate your thoughts and have a conversation about the issues. Your teen is going to blame you for a lot of things. That is part of being a parent to a teen. It doesn't really matter whether they are right or not; it's how you move forward from there. They probably believe they are right. It is their experience of what happened. It feels real to them. So find a way to soothe their anger, show understanding and empathy, and find solutions to move forward.

Don't Do It Alone

Parenting a teen is hard. Some parents feel like they just want to "give up" and let it be what it will be. They might even think that it's too late to fix any of it or they have run out of energy. This is where your support system is so important. Find your "cheerleader" to help you. This can look different for everyone (friend, partner, neighbor, therapist, etc.), but if you don't have that already, it is important to build your support.

If you are working with a partner and find you are often not on the same page, it is going to make this process a lot harder. Learning good communication and parenting skills, as a team, is very important. A critical or passive partner can influence a teen negatively.

Passivity and criticism are not productive forms of communication. Couples' counseling might be necessary to get on the same page as your partner. This will strengthen your power as parents. As you develop those communication skills, your teen may notice and learn from watching you. Other resources might include a close relative, the parent of another teen who can relate to what you are going through, an empty nester who has successfully navigated the teen years and is willing to listen to and share with you, a neighbor or friend who can listen well and give you encouragement, or a therapist who works with families and teens.

Self-Care Is Not Selfish

It's necessary to talk about self-care. What you model and give will impact greatly how well this will all work out. Some people struggle with self-care because they think it's selfish. Self-care is different than selfish behavior. Selfish behavior means knowingly meeting your own needs by taking away from other people. Self-care behavior means knowingly meeting your own needs without taking away from others and allowing yourself to give back more in return. Here are examples that illustrate the difference between self-care and selfish behaviors: You have decided to take a painting class to further your passion and interest. The class is offered in the evening when there is nothing regularly scheduled, but you know that issues often "pop up" during the evening time, so you feel like you should stay home "just in case." Taking this class would be practicing self-care because it will help to replenish your physical, emotional, and spiritual self without taking away from another person. This class would allow you to come home more relaxed and ready to enjoy and share your artwork with your family. Now, in the same example, if you have decided to take the same class for the same reasons but you know the class is during a time in which you have already committed to bringing your teen to an activity and decide to tell your teen to cancel her activity so that you can go to your class, this might be a selfish act.

If you are not taking care of yourself and are just giving to your kids, then you are giving them the tired, worn-out version of you. If you are spending some time doing the things you like and getting refreshed, then you are giving your kids the best version of you. It's important to have balance in your life.

TRY THIS
SELF-CARE FOR PARENTS

WEARING YOURSELF OUT AS A PARENT IS NEVER A GOOD IDEA. TO GIVE YOUR BEST AS A PARENT, YOU MIGHT NEED TO DEVELOP YOUR SELF-CARE SKILLS. SPENDING A DATE NIGHT WITH YOUR PARTNER, HANGING OUT WITH A GOOD FRIEND CHATTING ABOUT ANYTHING BUT PARENTING, WORKING OUT, GOING FOR A WALK IN NATURE, TAKING A NAP, TAKING A DEEP DIVE INTO YOUR FAITH (GOING TO CHURCH/TEMPLE/SYNAGOGUE, PRAYING, MEDITATING, ETC.), JOURNALING, GOING TO THERAPY, EATING A HEALTHY MEAL, AND PLAYING SPORTS (GOLF, FISHING, SOCCER, RUNNING, ETC.) ARE ALL EXAMPLES OF SELF-CARE.

PICK SOMETHING THAT IS JUST FOR YOU AND DO IT THIS WEEK! REMEMBER, LOVING YOUR TEENS IS JUST PART OF WHO YOU ARE. PARENTING IS A JOB. SOMETIMES YOU NEED A BREAK TO BE MORE EFFICIENT AT YOUR JOB.

You got this

If you think experiencing your teen during this time is challenging, try to imagine what they are experiencing that has them behaving this way. The teen years are very challenging. Being willing to acknowledge their hard time will help you to view their behaviors as them needing you. Teens need their parents to create safety in a time when everything is changing for them. Most people hate change. Having clear boundaries and consistency can help them process their difficult emotions. If you get worn out and give up, they will most likely do the same.

If you are just learning how to set boundaries and are changing your parenting style, then be prepared for an adjustment that will take more effort. The first month will feel like a battle of wills. The past year or two has established a pattern your teen is used to, even if it wasn't healthy. As you learn new parenting skills and ways to connect with your teen, they might reject it at first. Remember, change is hard. As the backlash hits, lean in on the community you have built up, practice self-care, and keep going, so you can wake up the next day to do it all over again. Hold the boundaries and continue to be consistent even when it's hard.

Maintaining the hope and vision you have for a healthy relationship with your teen will help you through this time. Remember, your teen is not their behavior. They may make poor choices and may act in ways that are not so attractive, but they are reacting to life and may need new tools to cope. Developing those tools at home, before they leave to be an adult, can build your relationship. They are craving compassion, empathy, and structure. They may not realize it, but they also want your approval. Loving them where they are and cultivating good habits together is the best thing you can do to become closer and improve your relationship.

Try This
Know Your Resources

Be prepared by:

- Asking friends for book resources
- Knowing what trends are happening online
- Talking to other parents
- Talking to teachers

THRIVE and Parenting without Fear

Trust—It's important in this journey to trust your own resources and strengths.

Heal—Healing comes when everyone accepts people for who they are. Even accepting your own weaknesses can be powerful.

Respect—Respect their feelings as well as yours. Learn to manage your own so that you can model emotion management to your teen.

Invite—Some invitations come without words. Use your own behavior to invite them to change.

Validate—In this case, find validation among your peers to give you strength when parenting gets hard.

Enjoy—Enjoy moments for yourself so you can have a "full cup" to deal with your teen who may be struggling.

Chapter 3

FAMILY STRUCTURE

How is a family structure determined, and what role will your teen have in this structure? The twenty-first century has undergone some significant family structure changes. The traditional nuclear family is no longer the norm when it comes to family structure. It's more of a kaleidoscope of family styles. Today's families can be a nuclear family, blended family, co-parenting family, stepparent family, LGBTQ family, single-parent family, foster family, etc. It is the adults in the family who determine the structure based on their relationship choices in life. Who you choose to marry, live with, divorce, etc. will contribute to the role your teen will develop in your family? Children are often learning their roles and shaping their personalities based on the family structure. Regardless of who makes up your family structure, the goal of this chapter is to help you ensure a healthy family dynamic, healthy communication, and, above all, a safe family for your teen to thrive in.

How do you know what your family structure is and the role your teen is playing? The family structure is made up of the people living in your household and the people who come and go frequently enough to model behavior to your teens (partners, extended family, friends and neighbors, caretakers, etc.). It is also the boundaries established, the family rules and expectations, and how all this is modeled by the adults in the home.

In every family style, there are strengths and weaknesses. Some are uniform across all styles. One of your strengths include a desire to grow as a parent and learn better ways of interacting with your teen. You picked up a book on parenting; that's a good sign of wanting to learn. This potentially shows a desire to become a healthier and happier parent. Another strength includes the fact that you know your family better than anyone. This means you have the best insight on what will work and what won't. If you include respect, communication, and flexibility, you can make healthy adjustments to the family that work for you and your teen.

The possible weaknesses can include Internet overuse, financial struggles, anger management, people who are part of the structure who don't respect the boundaries, etc. If there is no clear leadership defined by the adults, the teen can become confused. If rules are not clarified and are inconsistent, it can cause anxiety, anger, and uncertainty for your teen. Behaviors are often repeated generationally and will likely continue unless there is an intentional effort to change the pattern. A common pattern that is often repeated generationally is yelling. If you were raised by parents who yelled a lot, there is a high probability that you are repeating this behavior with your children. A good indicator that this pattern is repeating would be to observe if your teen is yelling at you often. If the answer is "yes," pay attention to how often you are yelling at your teen. Your teen is probably behaving in the same way they are being taught by you. Please don't misunderstand this statement to mean that we condone your teen yelling at you; we are simply hoping to increase your awareness to see if you would like to make any changes in how you are communicating with your teen.

Try This
Family Art

Have your teen (or each kid in your family) create an art piece representing your family doing an activity. They can paint or use collage, and even crayons can be fun (or even mix it up). When they are done, ask them to tell you about the picture. Listen to the language they use. When you are looking at their art, ask yourself:

- How are the different people in the picture connected? Who is alone? Who is together?
- What is the mood of the picture? What colors and intensity are used?
- Even doing the project with half-interest will tell you something about how your teen feels about the family.
- Ask yourself, as the parent, how you feel about the picture.

This is a great way to get a subconscious view of your teen's mood about the family. Art often taps into the nonverbal part of the brain. Don't overthink this; it's just a fun way to start a conversation.

Family Structures

Some family structures have special considerations. This list is not exhaustive, and is just a simple overview, because even within each category, the possibilities are endless. You can potentially learn from each family type as you can incorporate their lessons into your life as well. Maybe you will encounter families struggling with different issues than you, as your teens will probably be more open to the brokenness of their friends' families. Showing compassion and building community is good for every family.

Traditional nuclear family

The traditional nuclear family has many strengths. Statistics have shown that having both parents at home in a *solid* marriage gives you an advantage. "Children living with both biological parents are 20–35% more physically healthy than children from broken homes" (Gillespie Shields Blog, 2016). "Being raised in a married family reduced a child's probability of living in poverty by about 82%" (Gillespie Shields Blog, 2016). This can be because they pay fewer caretaking costs or have dual incomes. In addition to financial and physical outcomes, parents in a nuclear family who share the same values and respect each other provide consistency and safety to their children and teens while they are growing up.

The traditional nuclear family can be an issue if the marriage is not sound. If the parent's relationship includes a lot of fighting and discord, you might have kids who grow up feeling unsafe and anxious. Another weakness might include when the nuclear family excludes extended family (Oelze, 2020) or outside influences, as this can lead to isolation and stress. Having a rich sense of community is important for a thriving teen. The final issue can be that nuclear families sometimes become too child centered and parents end up doing too much for their kids, not giving them opportunities to build grit or resiliency.

The best way to help your family thrive during some of these challenges might be to schedule family dinners inviting extended family members over once or twice a month or having people from your community of different generations join you for a meal. This is a great opportunity to agree to eliminate negative comments and communication during mealtime, keeping that time a safe space for families to spend together.

The stepparent family

Strengths in this family style can include a return to a two-parent household, which can help finances and parent support. There can also be an opportunity for the parents to model how to heal past relationship choices. Stepparents have a wonderful opportunity to provide additional love that is a choice. The stepparent joins the family and has an opportunity to show respect, nurturing, and guidance as an additional parent figure for the teen. They can choose to communicate with them, be flexible, and demonstrate respect. And what parent wouldn't be excited about their teen having another person in their life who can offer love and support. What a great gift.

The biggest challenge here is establishing the role of the stepparent. The role of a stepparent is not to replace the parent who lives in another household, but rather to bring additional love and support to your teen. A stepparent-teen relationship requires time to build a trusting and respectful connection. Just because a parent marries someone, it doesn't give them the right to immediately act as a parent, and your teen will be the first to tell you this. It is important for the family structure to include a role for the stepparent and gradually build up to being a part of the parenting dynamic. A great way to transition into this structure would be for the parent and stepparent to talk to their teen together and follow through with any discipline together. And for all stepparents out there in the world, we strongly encourage that you speak respectfully about the other parent in front of your teen. Regardless of the relationship you have with the other parent, that is still the teen's mother or father, and they deserve to be treated with respect for being the parent.

The single-parent family

Being a single parent is a huge challenge as it means one parent plays the role of two. The strength of this family structure is defined by the dedication and commitment of the single parent. Managing childcare and the work/home balance can become extremely draining, and having a romantic or social life sometimes gets put on hold or even forgotten. This family structure requires a lot of strength from the parent. It is important to remember that no person is an island, and the single parent can build their community to achieve the help and support they need. Often in single-parent families, the teen is more resilient and more likely to help with household chores out of necessity (Gillespie Shields Blog, 2016). It is important to be mindful that the teen does not become a second parent, especially when younger siblings are involved. It can be very easy to start relying on your teen to take care of and meet the needs of their younger siblings. There is certainly nothing wrong with giving your teens more responsibility, but as the parent, we would want to ensure that you are continuing to parent all your children, including your teen. A good way to monitor this is to set aside time each week in which your teen has time to pursue their own interest and spend time with friends.

Extended family

Extended family members may become guardians or primary caretakers in situations in which the primary parent is no longer able to care for their teen. These family members can consist of grandparents, siblings, aunts, uncles, or other extended family members. It is wonderful when extended family members can step in as a parent to help guide the teen in making healthy decisions. This can be a difficult role if the role is not clearly defined. The traditional "parent" title shifts, and someone else is the keeper of the rules and decision-making. The teen may feel like they are old enough to care for themselves and does not need any other guidance. It will be important to express to the teen that although this may be what they believe and feel, it will not stop you from providing structure and guidance in their new family. A huge benefit of this kind of family structure is having a broader understanding of family. It can sometimes also be an opportunity for your teen to develop a greater respect for the different generations.

Foster family

The strength and challenge to this type of family structure are the exact same, "love dished out." The significant amount of love that can be exchanged is the biggest heartbreak and the biggest reward of this type of family. Foster families often go through a lot of change. Saying goodbye to someone you have poured your heart into might feel like a mistake; however, to not pour your heart into anyone who is in your care would be a larger mistake. It doesn't matter if it's a week, a year, or "forever"; giving your all is a huge gift.

This family structure often requires a high level of patience, nonjudgmental attitude, and self-control. The trust factor is the largest hurdle for this family structure to navigate. Foster parents often appear repetitive and annoying to teens because there is a necessity of reviewing the structure and rules of the home. The consistency and follow-through offered by the foster parents allow for safety and trust to begin modeling consistent respect, choices, and open communication allow for any home to feel safe. This family structure has such a wonderful opportunity to bring support and love to a teen.

Adoptive family

We once met a man who was an adopted child who stated his parents always made him feel loved because he was told that being adopted made him "extra special." His adopted parents always told him the truth about being adopted, and they followed up this statement by telling him, "You are extra special because most parents have the child they give birth to, but we got to choose you as our child." As he grew up, other kids would tell him how sad it was that he was adopted, and he would reply, "Oh no, I'm sad for you. You were not special enough to be chosen." This is a great example of being honest with your child about adoption and allowing them to know how special they are to be your child.

The adoption process has expanded and evolved over the last twenty-five years beyond the traditional closed adoption. It is now a spectrum of adoptions from closed to open and international. Each type of adoption brings new opportunities, strengths, and challenges. As your adopted child becomes a teen, they may have more questions about their birth parents. We encourage you to not hear this as your teen not loving you as their parent, but rather your teen exploring their identity, which includes their genetics. The beauty of the adoptive family is the idea of being chosen to be part of the family while embracing where they come from. Celebrating that choice, for some, is a big event called the "Gotcha Day" (this is like a birthday celebration, but the whole family celebrates the day they "got" the adopted person and added them to their family).

TRY THIS
FAMILY DAY

CELEBRATING A SPECIAL DAY AS A FAMILY CAN BECOME A GREAT TRADITION AND A FUN WAY TO CELEBRATE AN OFF-SEASON. HERE ARE SOME PROMPTS TO HELP YOU DESIGN THE DAY:

- WHAT COLOR SCHEME WILL YOU CHOOSE, AND WILL PEOPLE DRESS IN THAT COLOR, OR WILL THERE BE DECORATIONS?
- WILL THERE BE A SPECIFIC MENU THAT BECOMES A TRADITION?
- WHAT ACTIVITIES CAN YOU PLAN THAT WILL FEEL LIKE A CELEBRATION?
- WILL YOU HAVE A "SOUNDTRACK" FOR YOUR DAY?
- WILL YOU BE DOING A GIFT EXCHANGE?

LGBTQ family

We are living in an era where relationship choices are becoming more accepted, and people are feeling more confident to openly share who they love without fear of facing discrimination. However, prejudice can still be a factor facing the LGBTQ community and LGBTQ family structures. This can be difficult for everyone in the family, but for teens who might lack confidence, discrimination may lead to significant depression. Finding support in your community and keeping the conversation open and honest with your teen can alleviate some of the anxiety and depression they may experience. A strength within this family structure is that your teen is growing up learning to be more accepting, inclusive, and compassionate toward others due to their life experiences.

Co-parenting family

Co-parenting has many challenges, primarily because separated parents need to work together to support their teen. The teen might have to maintain two sets of rules in two different households. In this family structure, co-parents need to practice open and honest communication to know when their teen might be struggling or when they might be manipulating. A teen might say, "I don't like your rules. I'm going to go live with my other parent." Sometimes this is a legitimate request from your teen seeking safety or sanity; other times, it can be a manipulation game they are playing to get what they want. The most successful co-parenting comes with learning great communication skills and behaving like adults. It means both heads of household sit down and collaborate on rule setting. Continue to support each other in raising your teen and maintain open communication. It's being consistent with the consequences and even supporting each other with the other household's rules and guidelines.

Realistically, this doesn't always happen. The top reasons for divorce are parenting, money, and sex. So what makes us feel that if parenting was the issue while married, it wouldn't still be the issue after your divorce? We are perfectly aware of this. We still want to encourage you to model and treat the other parent in the way you want your teen to treat adults in the family (including you). "Do as I say and not as I do" will no longer work for a teen. If you are dealing with a difficult dynamic, your job will be to speak respectfully about the other parent and not allow your teen to be placed in the middle of this dynamic. There may be times your teen may choose to stay with the other parent to get what they want, but remember your job is to prepare your teen to be the young adult you want them to be, and you can only do this with modeling good behaviors for them.

TRY THIS
TEEN PARENT

THIS EXERCISE IS ONLY IF YOU FEEL COURAGEOUS. ASK YOUR TEEN TO DESCRIBE THEIR PARENTING STYLE IF THEY WERE THE PARENT OF THE FAMILY. LISTEN TO THE PARTS THEY WOULD KEEP AND WHAT THEY WOULD TOSS. ASK WHAT RULES THEY WOULD ELIMINATE AND WHAT RULES THEY WOULD ADD. BE MINDFUL NOT TO JUDGE OR MAKE NEGATIVE COMMENTS. THIS IS JUST A GREAT WAY TO GATHER INFORMATION. IF THERE IS TENSION DURING THE CONVERSATION, TRY TO INJECT SOME HUMOR INTO IT (BE OKAY WITH LAUGHING AT SOME OF YOUR WEAKNESSES).

Understanding your Family Structure

As you can see, there are many family structures. In every situation, you are the one who holds the boundaries of the family and guides your teen in their role within the family. Each of these family structures allows for strengths and opportunities to build communication and establish healthy boundaries. They all benefit teens with a clear definition of roles. There are also areas that can be improved upon in every family. It is the courageous parent who is willing to really look at their family and take responsibility to secure the health of their family.

THRIVE and Family Structure

Trust—Trust that no matter what choices are in your past as a parent, you can move toward a better relationship with your teen if you start now.

Heal—Healing comes from accepting that your past is just that, the past. Healing can only come from moving forward.

Respect—Respect that you will be different than all other families, even if you share a similar structure.

Invite—Invite your family to move forward and not stay stuck in anything that is toxic or broken

Validate—Don't look left and right, but only at yourself and validate where you are now.

Enjoy—Whatever your family structure, find occasions to celebrate your own experience.

Chapter 4

PARENTING STYLES

A healthy family structure has the parents clearly defining the expectations and rules for your teen. All members of the family structure are aware of the rules and support your decision, regardless of if they agree with them or not. For example, grandparents, stepparents, and older siblings will all echo the same decision. So how do you know if your rules demonstrate healthy boundaries? You don't…yet. But there are ways to explore that.

When considering all these things, we have found there are five main types of parents. There are the helicopter parent, the checked-out parent, the friend parent, the drill sergeant, and the consultant.

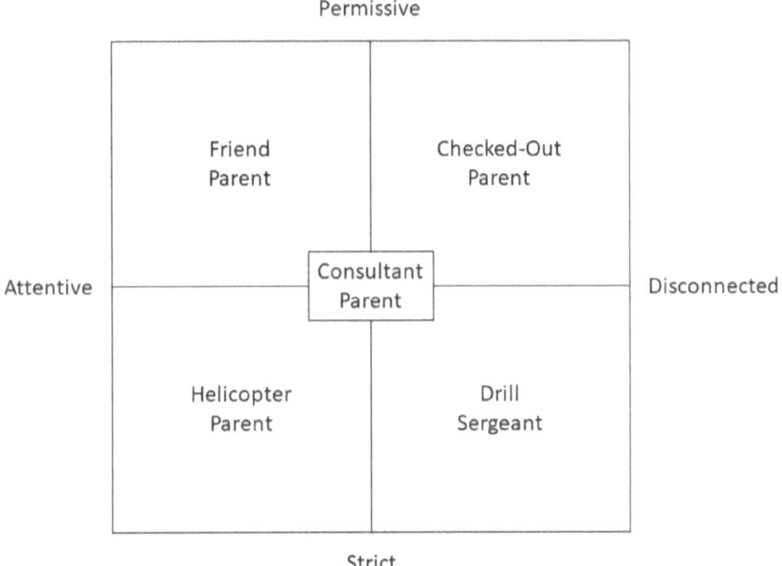

The helicopter (or snowplow) parent

This is the parent who hovers like a helicopter, hence the name. WebMD defines the snowplow parent this way: "Snowplow parenting, also called lawnmower parenting or bulldozer parenting, is a parenting style that seeks to remove all obstacles from a child's path so they don't experience pain, failure, or discomfort. However, these experiences are crucial for healthy childhood development and help children learn important life skills" (WebMD, 2021).

Helicopter parenting can seem like an attractive option. It may feel like you are helping your child avoid uncomfortable feelings and protecting them from difficulty. Your child will never have to wrestle with boredom or losing (like losing a game). Every minute is supervised and carefully controlled. These are the kids who take a million classes from music to art to dance to SAT classes. The parent books their teen's life full of carefully chosen activities preventing any chances of failure.

These kids often lack grit. They may succeed in some ways, but they can struggle to make decisions on their own. They rarely take risks because they have not had to recover from failure. They also tend to have anxiety. They grow up thinking that performance is everything. When they do struggle with something (even at the college level and beyond), they come back to their parent asking to be "bailed out" of any problem. These are the parents who work harder than their teen at everything (like getting into the right college).

At the extreme edge of this parenting style are "urban legend" like stories that go around, of parents showing up at job interviews with their teen or going to a college and speaking up for their teen to a professor, or a parent showing up in their teen's boss' office and demanding something. These are the snowplow parents. They struggle to let their kids make decisions on their own because they don't want their child to fail.

Teens raised in this environment tend to struggle in making decisions for themselves. They often struggle to solve their own problems and are constantly seeking the approval of their parents or others. This dynamic can lead to unhealthy adult relationships as they try to find others to make their decisions for them.

The checked-out parent

The checked-out parent is completely uninvolved. Whether it is their need to focus only on themselves or they are so overwhelmed with work and the struggles of their own life, they have stopped parenting. This is the opposite of the helicopter parent. They assume their kids will "be fine" if they leave them to their own devices. These parents pay little attention to their teen's needs or struggles. They rarely know where their teen is and who they are hanging out with.

These teens are often looking for acceptance as they have yet to figure out their own self-worth. Without the supervision and guidance of an active parent, they attach themselves quickly to anyone willing to accept them as they are. As young adults, their relationships can be plagued with chaos and neediness, often leading to various cycles of abuse. They would prefer to stay in an unhealthy relationship than be alone.

In the 1980s movie *Breakfast Club*, Allie Sheedy's teen character famously talks of how bad it is at home. She's distraught and crying.

In the end, she explains, "They ignore me" (Hughes, 1985). Teens rarely thrive when they don't have love, respect, and support. They almost can't survive without any kind of parenting. This environment needs support from the outside. Teachers, pastors, family, and other parents are the people who this kind of parent should reach out to, to gain the support needed for proper safety.

TRY THIS
ATTENTIVE OR DISCONNECTED?

FIRST, TAKE SOME TIME TO REMEMBER BACK TO YOUR OWN TEEN YEARS. WHAT WAS YOUR EXPERIENCE WITH YOUR PARENTS? DID THEY PAY ATTENTION TO YOU? DID THEY HOVER? DID THEY IGNORE YOU? WHAT DID YOU FEEL ABOUT HOW THEY TREATED YOU? REALLY BE AWARE OF YOUR OWN EXPERIENCE.

OBSERVE YOUR BEHAVIOR FOR A WEEK. DO YOU PARENT LIKE YOUR PARENTS? DO YOU DO THE OPPOSITE? HOW OFTEN DO YOU SOLVE YOUR TEEN'S PROBLEMS? HOW OFTEN DO YOU DO THINGS FOR THEM SO THEY ARE NOT UNCOMFORTABLE? ARE YOU HEARING THEM? HOW OFTEN DO THEY HAVE TO SAY YOUR NAME BEFORE THEY GET YOUR ATTENTION? *OBSERVE*!

The friend parent

The friend parent is permissive. They hate to say, "No," to their teen because they want to avoid conflict and hope to find acceptance from their teen. They are afraid to look like "the bad guy." So they allow their kids to have all their wants granted. It can feel like you get to have a friendship with your teen. Unfortunately, this parenting style also often lacks boundaries and often leaves your teen feeling unsafe. One example of this parenting style is the adult who buys alcohol or weed for their teen and their friends.

Friendship is a mutual relationship in which people share experiences and support. If you consider yourself as your teen's friend, that will indicate that not only is your teen sharing thoughts, feelings, and information with you but also in return, you are sharing your thoughts, feelings, and information with your teen. This is where the boundaries become blurred, and you are no longer in the parent role. Parenting a teen should be a one-way friendly relationship in which you offer guidance and support to your teen.

Teens with this kind of parent often struggle to set their own boundaries because they have not seen them modeled. Teens need clear boundaries. It gives them a container to take risks in and still make safe choices. A parent who has a consistent, reasonable "no" will be teaching their teen safe boundaries. They too will learn to say "no."

The "friend parent" style often lacks safety, leading to teens feeling nervous and insecure. They feel the weight and responsibility of their parent's need for acceptance. This can create anxiety and numbing behaviors. In adult relationships, these teens tend toward people pleasing and codependency.

The drill sergeant

The drill sergeant can sometimes be called the authoritarian parent. They are strict and rigid in their parenting style. Mistakes are seen as failure, and consequences can sometimes be harsh. Their main goal is to have their teen's respect through the use of control.

Often, in this parenting style, anger and fear are the driving forces of the relationship. Parents don't want to hear any opinions, and they certainly don't want to be disrespected. They expect their teen to accept their authority and do what they say. Teens who experience this style of parenting often respond with anger and rebellious behaviors.

It's true that teens of this kind of parent will most likely behave when that drill sergeant is present. The minute the parent is gone, they are likely to misbehave if they think they can get away with it. They might test other guardians, like teachers, to see if they can get away with negative behavior. They are also more prone to sneaking around and hiding their mistakes.

Some of the strengths of this parenting style can include consistency and clear rules, and everyone seems to know the household expectations and who is in charge. Unfortunately, this kind of parent, at their worst, are bullies. This may set your teen up to be a bully or even be bullied. "What the new study shows is that both engaging in bullying behavior and being the victim of bullying behavior are potential consequences of a parenting style that includes mockery, derision, and a lack of emotional support and empathy for the feelings of the child" (Whyte, 2021).

The teen in this style or parenting probably does not feel heard. They don't feel empowered to make their own choices and may spend the bulk of their life asking people's opinions when they need to make any kind of decision. The other sad outcome is that they may become a bully as a parent as well. Often, parenting styles are repeated by their children, or they go to the opposite, which, in this case, would be the friend parent (also not a healthy style of parenting as we have discussed).

TRY THIS
PERMISSIVE OR STRICT?

INDULGENCES ARE NICE THINGS UNTIL THEY'RE OVERDONE (ONE CHOCOLATE VERSUS THE WHOLE BOX). STRUCTURES AND RULES CAN BE HELPFUL UNTIL THEY'RE OVERDONE. BEING RIGID OR INCONSISTENT ABOUT FAMILY LIFE IS NOT HEALTHY. OBSERVE YOUR PARENTING FOR A WEEK AND JOURNAL WHEN YOU WERE CONSISTENT AND WHEN YOU WERE FLEXIBLE. BE AWARE OF YOUR MOTIVES FOR YOUR FLEXIBILITY OR CHOICE NOT TO BE. FOR EACH EXAMPLE, WRITE DOWN THE FEELINGS BEHIND YOUR DECISION, THE THOUGHTS THAT MOTIVATED YOUR CHOICE, AND THEN REFLECT ON WHETHER YOU THINK IT WAS A HEALTHY OPTION FOR YOU AND YOUR TEEN.

The consultant

Collaboration, collaboration, collaboration! This parenting style is marked by mutual respect and clear communication with the whole family. This parent has found the middle ground between being attentive and disconnected. These parents spend time together at meals, having open conversation about life. They help their teen use critical thinking to make life choices. They not only participate with them when asked but also give them room to build resiliency by giving them the space to struggle, be bored, and even make mistakes they can learn from.

Another balance you will see here is a safe option between strict and permissive. The goal is for consistency. The rules include clear expectations with a pinch of grace. Most of the rules have been discussed as a family, and logical consequences are clearly defined. The consequences might include positive incentives, fair outcomes, and age-appropriate punishment. "You spilled the milk. No need to freak out. Here's a cloth. Please clean it up."

This style of parenting rarely includes yelling. The parents have a relationship with their kids, but it is based on a parent/child structure with all the roles unmistakably defined and a strong sense of mutual respect. This is the kind of parenting most discipline books are writing about. The parent is asking their teen for their thoughts and opinions, talking to others involved, and weighing the pros and cons. This provides the parent with the best possible outcome at that time.

For example, your teen wants to go "hang out" with some new friends, which leaves you feeling uncomfortable. In a consultant parenting style, you would obtain all the logistical information for the night. How long will they be out, who exactly is going, where will they be hanging out, etc. If you have never heard of these friends, you might ask about how they met, if they make good choices, and how you could get in touch with their parents if you needed to. Based on all these responses from your teen, you would then make your decision. But wait, what if you find out later that one of these friends brought alcohol or drugs to share with your teen? Well, you will now use this new information to make different decisions moving forward. This should happen during the early years of high school so that by the time they are seniors and close to graduating, you know you can trust them when they say, "I'm going out with my friends."

The consultant is flexible, respectful (and usually has earned their teen's respect), a good communicator (including great listening skills), and consistent. They are prepared to discuss difficult situations and process with the family. They help their teen face their mistakes and problem solve, teaching growth and recovery from their errors. They are equipping their teen to become a responsible adult. This style of parenting grows with their teen. As they build trust and critical thinking, they can give their teen more freedom and more responsibility.

TRY THIS
FAMILY SCULPTING

THIS IS AN EXERCISE OFTEN USED IN FAMILY THERAPY. HAVE ONE TEEN (THE SCULPTOR) FROM YOUR FAMILY. PLACE EACH FAMILY MEMBER IN A POSITION AROUND THE ROOM BASED ON HOW THEY SEE THAT FAMILY MEMBER. ONCE EVERYBODY IS PLACED, IT SHOULD LOOK LIKE EVERYONE IS A STATUE. MAYBE A PARENT IS AT THE COMPUTER OR ON THE PHONE. MAYBE A LITTLE SIBLING IS POSITIONED CLOSE TO A PARENT TRYING TO GET THEIR ATTENTION. ONCE EVERYONE IS PLACED, THE SCULPTOR SHARES THE REASONS FOR HIS PLACEMENTS AND ASKS THE FAMILY MEMBERS TO SHARE HOW THEY FEEL ABOUT HOW THEY WERE POSITIONED.

Skill Building

Your parenting skills are defined by your value system and the young adult you are helping to create. Listening, flexibility, and role modeling are the cornerstones to improving those parenting skills.

Listening

Listening is probably the most important skill as a parent, and it is not as simple as it sounds. When therapists are working with couples or families, many of us will teach "reflective listening" or "active listening." Just because you hear your teen, it doesn't mean you are actively listening. If you ask any troubled teen, they will almost always state, "No one ever listens to me."

Teens will come to you many times in their relationship with you to complain, unload their frustrations, or even just debate an issue they think is unfair. The human instinct when people have someone speaking at them is to defend themselves, explain what they think is the truth, or go for the quick apology when they realize they may be wrong. This is the "quick fix" that may leave your teen unsatisfied and potentially grumpy.

If when your teen is coming to speak to you, it's a bad time, let them know a better time. Be specific, so they don't have to wonder when "later" is. "I want to give you my full attention. Can we talk right after dinner?" Giving them your full attention can be important. Put your phone down, step away from the computer, stop whatever you are doing, and really listen to what they have to say.

When they start sharing with you, occasionally summarize what they are saying or ask for clarification. "Am I understanding you right when you say…?" Look for moments where you can share you understand their point of view. You don't have to agree with them. "I can understand why it may seem unfair that I won't let you go to the dance. I know it must be disappointing, but you were told if you didn't turn in all your homework, then you would not go. I know this can't be a surprise to you, but I understand why you are upset."

Any situation where they don't get their way will be frustrating. Doesn't it bother you when you don't get your way? Give them a little understanding, but still maintain boundaries. "I can see you are angry with me. I can imagine not getting to go to the dance can be very infuriating. We did agree to these conditions, and the punishment stands. When you are ready to discuss what happened with your homework, I'm open to listening." Don't automatically fix it; just listen. Offer to be there but wait for them to ask for solutions. When working on solutions, help them brainstorm their own ideas.

As an adult, they need to learn to problem solve on their own. They need to understand how to think critically through their issues. Sometimes, their discomfort can be a learning experience. I (Stephanie) have a son who, in the first week of college, forgot his homework on his desk at home. He called to let me know. I could have driven it to him because his school was close. Instead, I said, "That sucks. I bet you figure it out." He talked to his teacher. He got a pass and never forgot his homework on his desk again. He also got an A in that class.

Listening is not agreeing with them but honoring that they need to be heard. To really make sure that you hear them, stop thinking about your answer, your solution, your rebuttal, your defense, your truth, and just hear them. Their version might sound false, but imagine if that is the way they see it. We all have different filters. Be willing to put yourself in their shoes.

In short, stop and listen. Don't think about your own agenda, but think about how they might be feeling, even if it is irrational. Ask for clarification. Summarize their points and show understanding. Once they feel heard and validated, defensiveness tends to decrease, and it becomes easier to have an open dialogue. If they are not demonstrating good listening skills, don't go to their level, continue to model proper communication, and eventually they will learn from that.

> ## TRY THIS
> ## DELEGATE!
>
> HAVE YOUR TEEN TAKE ON SOME TASKS AROUND THE HOUSE. MAYBE THEY CAN DESIGN THE WEEK'S MENU, MAYBE THEY CAN COOK A MEAL FOR THE FAMILY, MAYBE THEY CAN PICK THE MOVIE FOR "FAMILY MOVIE NIGHT," MAYBE YOU CAN PUT THEM IN CHARGE OF GETTING OUT THE DOOR ON TIME (FOR CHURCH, FOR SCHOOL, ETC.), OR MAYBE PUT THEM IN CHARGE OF PLANNING AN OUTING FOR FUN—BE CREATIVE. NOT ALL CHORES HAVE TO BE NEGATIVE. THINK OF SOMETHING THEY WOULD ENJOY AND PUT THEM IN CHARGE.

Flexibility

We've acknowledged you will make errors and are growing and learning from them. So are your kids. You are both maturing and developing. That means the rules need to be flexible—not the kind of flexible where you can be talked out of a punishment, but the kind of flexible that considers growth.

Sitting down and having family meetings to review the rules occasionally is a smart idea. Some things to consider when being flexible are:

- Are the rules working?
- Are there any opportunities to adjust the rules?
- Has your teen taken the rules seriously and earned some freedoms?

These types of questions show a willingness to change and/or compromise within the family system. This encourages an ongoing, open dialogue, which builds respect.

Role modeling

You are going to make mistakes (just like your teen). You might be applying your new listening skills but get frustrated and blow up. If you yell or something along those lines, it's time to be a role model again and show your teen how to recover. Blame never works, so avoid any sentence that starts with "You made me…" No one can make you do anything.

If you were angry, you had a choice to communicate your anger calmly. If you yelled, that is also your choice, so own it. "I'm sorry I yelled. I'm still angry you behaved that way, and there will still be consequences, but I should not have yelled. Let's talk again when I feel a calmer." Taking responsibility to behave like an adult is hard. It means owning your mistakes and being humble enough to apologize properly and be accountable (we'll explore further the proper apology in the next chapter).

All parents make mistakes. Have some compassion for yourself. Making mistakes is an opportunity, not a door closing. Since everyone does it, role modeling how you recover is what shows a person's character.

The Unexpected

Sometimes, life comes along and flips the whole family upside down. Some of these events are good; some are not. Some things the parents might have control over like divorce, moving, graduation, new partner, job change, pregnancy, addiction recovery, etc. Some are external circumstances that no one has control over like a death in the family, financial crisis, layoffs from work, family illness, loss of property, and pandemic lockdown. You parents are certainly not always to blame, but here's the thing—you are responsible. As the adult in the family, it is on you to guide your family. It is on you to create safety.

What does it look like to take responsibility? You might be feeling the discomfort of change and struggling to keep a level head. It might be a really hard time for you. An example is divorce. The parent might be feeling the loss and fear of it all. They wonder why their teen is making it worse by acting up. STOP! Divorce is never about just the couple. If you are feeling off, then you should just assume your teen is too. Telling them, "It's not about you," is not enough. This is true of most big family events.

Teens are smart enough to know when their parents are lying. They know when things are not going well. That being said, they can easily misunderstand how they are "responsible" or how the big events will impact them. Being honest and sharing appropriate information with your teen can soothe their worries. Getting through these extreme times is all about communication and making sure the teen in your life knows what is going on. Give them opportunities to have control over some choices when things are changing drastically. Include them in the discussions and hear their input. It doesn't mean doing what they want. It means listening for their struggle and making sure you are equipping them for the changes.

Remember the family structure is determined by you, the parent, so how you choose to communicate and interact with your teen will help guide them down the path that you are creating. With so many types of family structures today, it is so important to acknowledge how your teen is feeling about the structure and their role within the family. And how you choose to parent will determine to what level of success your teen will become a confident, independent, and healthy adult.

THRIVE and Parenting Styles

Trust—It's important to trust this process. Becoming the consultant parent is not always the easiest choice, but it provides for the healthiest outcome for your teen.

Heal—Healing can happen at any time. It's never too late to make changes and rebuild relationships. Learning flexibility and consistency and how to balance that in the heathiest way takes time.

Respect—Two things that kill the average teen's respect for their parents are (1) parents trying too hard to be their friend or, conversely, (2) parents demanding their teen's respect without respecting them.

Invite—Invite your teen to speak their heart (respectfully) and remember to listen reflectively.

Validate—Everyone's emotions are valid and deserve to be heard using healthy communication

Enjoy—Enjoy the collaboration process with your teen as it will build relationship.

Chapter 5

TALKING WITH YOUR TEEN

The last chapter we examined how family structure impacts a family and the roles everyone plays. Let's talk about the practical part of connecting with your teen. If in the past your interactions have been filled with eye rolls, sarcasm, and yelling, it might be time to woo your teen's heart back. Maybe you have a great relationship with your child but have been a little hesitant heading into the teen years. We will go into more detail in a later chapter about hormones and major events that can make a teen moody. We'll also explore more about individuation, which can cause rebellion. We've talked about roles and responsibilities and how changes and confusion can cause a teen to act out. Let's talk about repairing broken relationships or transitioning to parenting a teen instead of a child.

Some warnings are needed. LOCATION, LOCATION, LOCATION is everything. Discussing family issues in public places or in front of other people (friends, family, neighbors. etc.) is inappropriate. To show that you are taking this seriously, it will benefit you to find a safe place without intruding ears (or mouths). You would not want your boss to talk to you in front of the whole company. These discussions are private (please keep them off social media). Remember to find your calmest and sweetest voice possible. We call it the "honey voice." It's called that because it should be as sweet as honey and might even start with "Honey, can we talk?"

Repairing the Past

If your teen is hesitant to talk with you, you may want to repair some of the damage, in this relationship, they feel has happened in the past. The first step is owning and repairing anything you may have done to add to the strife, even if there was no intention of causing trouble at all. You are the adult in the relationship, so you will be the one starting the ball rolling in the right direction. The first step is not an apology (we'll get to that); it's hearing what the problem is. *"I know we have not been getting along lately, but I would like to fix that. I would like us to build mutual respect. I think that starts with me hearing from you and how you think things are going."*

This is the hard part. LISTEN. Actively listen without defending or explaining. This is the consultant parenting style and an opportunity to model to your teen how you would like to be heard. Listening is hard. Most humans have the instinct to say things like "That's not how it happened." They want to correct their teen's version of events. Or they might say, "That was not what I meant when I said that." They want to fix misinterpretations right away. It is very hard not to try to use logic and reframing to make things right. THIS WILL PROBABLY NOT WORK. What they hear when you do that is, "I'm not listening to you because you are wrong." What they need is the validation that their version is being respected. Respecting their version is a great start to winning back their heart (even if their version seems out of this world). So bite your tongue, take a deep breath, and just listen.

If they are getting angry, first do a quick self-check that you aren't reacting, instead of listening. If you are in a power struggle, stop and go back to listening. If their anger is habit, remind them "You don't need to yell. You have my full attention." This might be a new concept to them. Give them time to change.

Allow for some silences. If they say things like "I don't know" as a response to your questions, give them time to think. You might even say, "Okay, I will give you time to think about it while I sit here and wait," and then sit quietly. Your body language will be communicating a lot to them, so face them and try to relax your whole body. Be aware of facial expressions.

An action that can be helpful is to maybe write down the key points they are sharing. This gives your brain something to do. Because they are not little children, your responses to their words and behavior don't have to be instant. If you feel yourself getting angry, take a break and say, "I'm going to go think about what you have said, and we can talk again in a little while."

While you are processing what they have shared, take a look at the part you played in their struggle. Some possibilities are:

- You do not really understand their side.
- You have been distracted by your own stressors.
- You had to make some big changes in the family to adjust to some life circumstances.
- You have a short fuse and have little patience.
- You are still learning about parenting.

Whatever they are upset about, it's important that they feel heard. Remember, feeling heard is not saying they are right. Sometimes they will complain about things that don't make sense. You may, in fact, not be "to blame" for any of the trouble in the family, but you are the adult taking *responsibility* for repairing the relationship. That is what being the adult is about.

TRY THIS
LETTING GO OF ANGER

SOMETIMES YOU WILL HAVE A DIFFICULT TIME WITH YOUR TEEN AND MAY NOT GET A SINCERE APOLOGY. LEARNING TO LET GO OF YOUR ANGER IS A GREAT SKILL, SO YOU DON'T HAVE TO BE IN A REACTIVE MOOD. SOME OF THE FOLLOWING ARE SOME GREAT WAYS TO PRACTICE LETTING GO OF YOUR ANGER.

- SHARE YOUR FEELINGS WITH A FRIEND.
- VALIDATE YOUR ANGER BY TAKING A MINUTE TO ACCEPT THAT YOU HAD A RIGHT TO BE ANGRY.
- JOURNAL YOUR THOUGHTS.
- TAKE SOME DEEP BREATHS.
- MEDITATE.
- EXERCISE, LIKE GOING FOR A WALK.

MODELING THIS WILL SHOW YOUR TEEN HOW TO MANAGE ANGER.

STEPS TO GOOD APOLOGY

An apology is tricky. Some people think they are apologizing but may be making it worse. There are a few things to avoid in a proper apology. It is not as simple as "I'm sorry" and you are done. It's also being careful not to apologize for your teen's feelings, "I'm sorry you are upset." That might be the beginning of the next battle (think about how it would make you feel if your teen said "Sorry you're mad"). It's a bit dismissive and can be seen as condescending. There should be no blame in an apology like, "You made me angry" (remember, you are responsible for your own feelings and responses). What is a good apology, you ask?

1. Being genuine

Don't say something you don't mean. Teens have an ability to sniff out the…well…lies. To find your genuine voice means that you took time to listen to your teen. You are looking at what part you played in their frustration or anger. You are taking into account their version of the events (even if they are very different from yours). Remember that their version is their reality. This also means letting go, for a little while, to your version of the story (This is hard for EVERYONE). You are giving up the need to be "right" so that you can repair the dialogue.

2. Taking responsibility and expressing regret

Once you have pinpointed the issue, it's time to take responsibility. You are not saying they are right and you are wrong. Taking responsibility means that you care about their experience, and you are truly sad they are struggling. The apology might look like:

- "I can see why you thought I was not understanding you. I'm sorry I didn't better communicate with you about this topic."
- "I'm sorry I have not been paying attention to you lately. I can see how I have let my own stress get in the middle of our relationship."
- "I'm sorry that our lives have been so upside down lately. I have had to make some hard choices, but I probably didn't do the best job of helping you through this difficult time. I bet this is hard for you."
- "I'm sorry I yelled. I should not yell at you. I am still angry at what happened, AND I own that I could have reacted better."

Look closely and notice the language includes being the adult in the situation. You can see how taking responsibility is the building block to showing your teen respect and earning it from them.

Some of these apologies include validating your teen and their experience and feelings. Again, validation does not mean that they are right. It means that they have a right to their feelings. There is a big difference. It is in regaining the dialogue, you can help them eventually change their interpretation of their feelings and take adult actions honoring them. This is not about being right or winning; it's about growth and respect. What a great opportunity to model the kind of behavior you would want to see in your teen if they were someday parenting their own kids.

3. Moving forward with accountability

This is the part where you state how your actions will be different in the future. You will want to share how you will be changing your behavior. There is a difference between responsibility and accountability. Responsibility is acknowledging your behavior and apologizing. Accountability is acknowledging and stating how you will change your behavior moving forward. Some examples are:

- "I am sorry for not letting you finish your thoughts. I want to hear what you have to say. Can we spend some time just talking calmly together? I will listen to what you are saying."
- "I am going to work on managing my stress. I plan to begin practicing meditation. You are invited to practice with me. It might help both of us."
- "I feel bad everything is so crazy lately. Maybe we could spend some one-on-one time together. Maybe go for some ice cream or something to just take a break. I can't promise things will get easier right away, but I want to know how I can help you through this hard time."
- "I am sorry for yelling at you. I would not appreciate someone yelling at me. I am going to read some books on healthy communication. I don't want to be the parent who yells."

4. Making requests and taking action

The basic request you can make is simply finishing up by asking "Do you forgive me?" Some people appreciate being asked. If your teen is really in a state of anger, it's okay if they say, "No." If that is the case, try, "Okay. I understand. This has been hard. I hope you can forgive me some day." Give them time to catch up with you. You have been reading about this and contemplating this for a bit. They have had only a few minutes to get used to you making changes and building respect. It might also be important to remember that some of your relationship habits have been building for over a decade. If you are trying to make a change, give it time.

Let your teen know that you are going to be actively working on improving your parenting style. "I want to be a better parent, and I want us to have a better relationship. I hope we can strengthen our relationship to show each other more respect. I will probably make mistakes, and I'm sorry for that. As you know, I'm not perfect. I will continue to make every effort to be a healthy parent." The more vulnerable you are about your imperfect parenting, the more you let them know it's normal to make mistakes and correct them. It is not a sign of weakness, but a sign of humility.

Just because you apologized, it does not mean you "owe" your teen any kind of restitution or favor. Guilt about making mistakes as a parent is only helpful for about two minutes. Let it be your inner voice letting yourself know you erred. Then use that information to get back on track. You can't change the past; you can only move forward. Sometimes an apology will even include consequences for your teen. For example, let's say they broke a rule. You yelled. Now it's time to say, "I'm sorry I yelled at you. I know that was not right. I am still angry with what you did, and there will still be consequences. I need time to calm down, and then we can talk about what will happen next."

It is great to have these conversations with your teen about their grievances. It does not mean they can be disrespectful and critical of you at every turn. The first time you talk with them, they may be angry. As the discussions go forward, it's important to speak calmly (model that at every chance you get). If they have an issue, remind them if they are being disrespectful in their tone or attitude, "I do want to listen, but only if you are using a respectful tone and you have something constructive to share. It's not okay to just yell at me, whine at me, or complain. That is not productive. Do you want to sit and have a respectful conversation?"

TRY THIS
DINNER TALK

PRINT A BUNCH OF CONVERSATION STARTERS FOR YOUR FAMILY (WE'VE INCLUDED AN EXAMPLE OF QUESTIONS IN APPENDIX A). I (ANGELE) HAVE THEM IN A BOWL ON THE DINNER TABLE. MY STEPSON, A HIGH SCHOOLER, PICKS ONE AND READS IT ALOUD AT THE TABLE. EVERYONE GETS A CHANCE TO ANSWER. THIS IS A GREAT TIME TO FIND WAYS TO DISAGREE RESPECTFULLY OR EVEN MODEL LISTENING SKILLS.

Building Communication

Wooing your teen's heart back is more than just an apology. It means building new and positive memories. It's learning the skills of communication to make future encounters more productive. In counseling, communication might be one of the top skills we teach. You would think talking would be simple since you have been doing it your whole lives. The words, tone, and body language you choose will all make an impact on how people perceive you.

If someone yells, "Do your chores," and someone else says the exact same words using a sweet singsong voice, you will get different results. If you smile and ask your teen a question, you will have a different outcome than if you are a person who scowls and asks the exact same question.

TRY THIS
FIXING YOUR TONE

GET A VOICE RECORDER (MOST SMARTPHONES CAN DO THIS). RECORD YOURSELF SAYING THE FOLLOWING QUOTE, USING DIFFERENT TONES AND EMPHASIZING DIFFERENT WORDS. USE YOUR NORMAL TONE FIRST. THEN TRY ANGRY, CALM, BOLD, OR ANIMATED.

"I NEVER SAID TO DO THAT."

LISTEN TO YOUR RECORDING (EVEN BETTER IF IT'S A VIDEO). WHAT DO YOU NOTICE ABOUT HOW YOU SPEAK THOSE KINDS OF STATEMENTS? WHAT FELT COMFORTABLE? WHAT FELT RUDE? WAS THERE ONE THAT WAS CONFIDENT AND KIND?

SHOW YOUR TEEN WHAT YOU DID. IF YOU ARE DARING, ASK THEM WHAT SEEMS CLOSEST TO HOW THEY EXPERIENCE YOU, BUT ONLY IF YOU ARE PREPARED FOR THE ANSWER.

Basic building blocks

Now is the time to model relationship. It might feel easy to go back to old habits. You might have a long day, some bad news or some other trigger, and it sets you off to speak disrespectfully to your teen. Maybe they are coming at you with attitude. You might think a solid, stern, sharp statement will make it end (Hmm...did that work in the past?). If your teen snaps at you, you might feel irritated. Responding with irritation teaches irritation. However, responding in a calm voice, "Honey, I have had a long day. Can I have a little space, then we can talk in a little bit?" will be so much more powerful.

This means you need to model the other side of that as well. If you hear your teen stomp in the door and say, "Leave me alone! My day sucked." Then give them some space. Wait a little before checking in. When you do approach, maybe use your softest, most compassionate voice, "I'm sorry you are having a rough day. Let me know if you need me." Don't use that moment to add your own grievances or comments. Saying, "Don't slam the door," is not productive in this moment.

Timing

When you are asking them to join you for dinner, stop playing video games, get ready to leave, do their chores or any other transition, use the "fifteen-minute rule." This will be especially true if you are dealing with an introvert (love those deep thinkers), a video game fan (they need time to save and transition), or a teen on the spectrum (they really do want to know what is expected and need transition time)—really most humans appreciate a little heads up that things are going to change. Give them fifteen-minute notice:

- Dinner is in fifteen minutes.
- You have fifteen minutes left of computer time.
- Please get started on your chores in the next fifteen minutes.
- We're leaving in fifteen minutes.

Demanding "Now!" often starts fights (and some of those fights last longer than fifteen minutes…yikes). Giving your teen some transition space shows them respect. Again, think how you feel when others demand you do something "Now!" It doesn't feel good. It can feel jarring. This is another opportunity to model respect. (Don't you wish your boss was reading this?)

Let's talk semantics

When parents use a lot of "Why didn't you…" or "Why do you always…" or "You never…" the teen feels attacked and defensive. This will set you up for failure. There are a few words here that don't often work if used in the wrong context:

- <u>You</u>: Use "you" with caution. If you are approaching them about an issue, this word is accusing "You didn't do the dishes again." Another option is to say "I feel frustrated when the dishes don't get done at night. That's your responsibility. I'd like to talk about that." Can you hear the difference? In addition, "you" should be used for encouragement—"You did a great job on your chores. Thanks!"

- <u>Why</u>: "Why" often conveys judgment. It questions people's motivation. If your boss said, "Why are you late?" you might feel scolded. "What happened? You are not usually late." Feels a little more about curiosity than judgment. And do you really need to know why they didn't do the chores? "Why aren't the chores done?" This is an unproductive statement that can lead to arguments. A simple "I noticed the chores aren't done. Could you please get started on that?"

- <u>Never/always</u>: Absolutes are *never* a good idea (see what I did there). Using absolutes like "You never listen" will discount the power of your statement. "I need us to be respectful with each other like the conversation we had last week." Think of exceptions to your absolute statements. Use that for effect.

Humor

Laugh! Yes, laugh! Humor is so important to building a good relationship with your teen. Laugh at your own mistakes. Have family jokes. Laugh at the silly things that happen. I (Stephanie) was born and raised in Canada. When I mispronounce a word or give a reference to something no one seems to get, my whole family says, "Must be a Canadian thing." We all laugh (it's our thing). I (Angele) have crazy conversations at dinner that often start with a strange question like, "Who here would be the first to die in a zombie apocalypse and why?" Being creative and spontaneous can be very bonding and lighten the mood.

Don't tease your teen unless you have built up that kind of relationship. Don't make fun if you aren't also willing to laugh at yourself. If you are trying out some teasing, look for their reaction. If they don't laugh, stop. Please don't confuse sarcasm with humor. Think about how you feel when your teen uses sarcasm on you. It's biting and hurtful. Sarcasm can convey disrespect and condescension. The humor in your house should not have your teen as the butt of the joke. Humor that excludes the person being made fun of is called bullying.

Try This
Family Video

CREATE A FAMILY VIDEO. IT CAN BE A FAKE COMMERCIAL, A DANCE ROUTINE, OR MAYBE A FAVORITE MOVIE SCENE— WHATEVER THE CHOICE, GIVE YOUR TEEN THE JOB OF DIRECTING IT. SO MANY TEENS SEE LIFE ON THE INTERNET AND WONDER, *WHY ISN'T MY LIFE LIKE THAT?* GIVE THEM A TASTE OF SEEING THEIR OWN FAMILY ON SCREEN. THIS IS A GREAT OPPORTUNITY TO LISTEN, GIVE THEM FUN RESPON-SIBILITIES, AND WORK AS A FAMILY WHILE USING HUMOR.

Addressing Specific Issues with Your Teen

After using and practicing the building blocks, it might be time to start communicating the issues you are having with your teen in a productive way. No yelling. No blaming (at least on your part). This is how you not only rebuild your relationship but also establish safe boundaries and help your teen become a productive adult. They may not meet you in this new place of better communication skills. This is where the perseverance and patience become necessary. Keep modeling what you hope they will do. You can't have expectations of your teen to change into something unless you are modeling it for them.

Get the big picture

Before you address issues in your teen, you will want to first look at who they really are. Parents sometimes get overwhelmed at how often the teen goes through changes because it can happen quickly. Some parents want to take control of the changes. This will only lead to power struggles. Some think that every action their teen makes is a reflection of who they are as a parent, and they react out of embarrassment. Power struggles and embarrassment are only going to increase the issues.

Spend one week observing your teen through a different lens. Pay attention to their actions. What are they struggling with? If the words they were saying weren't about you, how are they feeling about the world and themselves? What is causing their anger? What scares them? What are they proud of? What are they trying really hard to work on? What have they given up on? Who do they listen to, and who listens to them? Who do they admire?

Look beyond the surface. The teen who draws disturbing art and wears all black can also be seen as an artist who is struggling with some inner feelings that might be scary to them. Really look at them with a compassionate eye. See past their errors and try to really understand their struggle. ALL PEOPLE MAKE MISTAKES AND ARE FLAWED! See their strengths and their potential.

After wrapping your mind around their beauty, flaws, passion, and chaos, can you accept them right now? Can you love them for who they are? Can you accept them as a separate person from who you are? Can this process of helping them with issues be about helping them become the best person they can be, rather than the best person you want them to be? This process of dealing with issues is about building them up and enhancing who THEY are.

Teens deal with a lot of expectations and judgment from their peers. Their inner conversation is also often pretty harsh. They are constantly in a state of "Am I accepted? Am I loved?" You could be the one voice they hear that has compassion and love for them. Are you willing to be that voice?

TRY THIS
INSPIRATION COLLAGE

CREATE A VISION BOARD. ANSWER THE QUESTION "WHAT DO I LOVE ABOUT MY TEEN?"

SUPPLIES:

- PICTURES OF YOUR TEEN, YOUNG AND OLD
- MAGAZINES OR PICTURES
- GLUE OR TAPE
- SCISSORS
- BIG SHEET OF PAPER

PLACE YOUR VISION BOARD IN A SPACE THAT WILL INSPIRE AND REMIND YOU THE REASON YOU ARE WORKING TO IMPROVE COMMUNICATION WITH YOUR TEEN.

Make a plan

Make a list of the issues you would like to address with your teen (homework, behavior, drinking and drugs, chores, friends, dating, etc.). We recommend using the SMART model to prepare for your talk with your teen. SMART goals are great for establishing new behavior. You might even write one or two for your parenting style or communication skills, which you can share with your teen, to show you are making changes too.

Here's how to use the SMART model. We will give you two examples to see the contrast between vague goals and SMART goals:

1. I want my teen to have a better attitude all the time.
2. I want my teen to get up on his own in a timely manner every weekday by October 1st.

<u>Specific</u>: In 1, it is a vague statement because what is a "better attitude"? In 2, you know exactly the expectation. The teen will be getting up on time on their own.

<u>Measurable</u>: In 1, there is no way of measuring someone's attitude. In 2, you will know it is working if your teen is on time for school and you no longer have to get them up.

<u>Achievable</u>: In 1, the topic is so general—the teen will not know where to start or what to focus on to achieve this goal. In 2, it is achievable because most adults can do this unless there is a sleep issue, in which case it might not be achievable.

<u>Reasonable</u>: In 1, it is not reasonable because it is vague and the absolute language "All the time" is overwhelming. In 2, it is reasonable because the expectations are all clearly stated.

<u>Timed</u>: Give it a due date so that you can have a reward or consequence.

Take the list you made of the issues you feel need addressing. Figure out specific expectations you might be having for the outcome of your talk. For some, this is the hard part—choosing where to start. It's hard because here's the rule: Pick only one issue! Put them in order of importance or intensity. You might want to start with something easy so you can give your teen an easy win.

Once you have picked the issue to address, make sure your SMART goal is very clear. Have some ideas you can present to your teen for possible rewards for achieving the goal. Be prepared to discuss the consequences of not following through. Having all these pieces will make negotiating the issue easier.

It is a good idea to think of times when your teen has achieved this goal in the past. This gives you an opportunity to share with them your belief in them. It eliminates from the discussion the "never" and "'always" and shows your awareness of their abilities. Instead of "You never get out of bed on time," you can discuss, "I remember the time you were going skiing with your friends, and you got up on your own. What do you think was helpful for getting you up?"

*****

The discussion

Invite your teen into a collaborative conversation. Start by sharing concerns. Give your teen the opportunity to let you know how they feel about the topic. Remember to share some of your positive observations about how they have succeeded in the past. Let them know they are not unseen. Share your heart and why you care about this goal. Be ready for any kind of negative reaction. Don't correct it. If you need to comment on it, then say something productive. "I can see this seems a bit much for you right now. I really am trying to improve our situation. To do that, I do need your input. So I hope we can talk about this right now."

Talk about the one issue you want to see improved. Use language that lets them know you are equipping them for the future. Let's use the example from above:

"We seem to fight every morning about getting you out of bed. I really want to stop the fighting and prepare you for when you leave home. I am no longer going to come wake you up. You are now responsible for getting ready on time. I know you can because you have done it before. If you are on time for school for a month, with no more than two "tardies," I think there should be some kind of reward. What do you think is a good reward? (discuss—These do not have to be elaborate. Sometimes their success is reward enough.)… Now, what if you don't follow through? If in a month you have more than two "tardies" at school and you aren't waking up, what should the consequence be? (Discuss—Keep in mind when you are discussing consequences, consider how their actions will affect the outside world. For example, in this case, their tardies may also have school consequences.) Okay, I think we have a plan. I will not be nagging you about this or reminding you. I trust you will be trying to stick to your word. I will check in in a month."

It's a lot easier if you have buy-in from your teen. If they agree to the "deal," then you might find them trying harder to change. If you are taking the approach that you decide what the plan is and what the results will be, then be sure they understand your expectations very clearly and understand the consequences. Either way, clarity, reasonableness, and follow-through will be crucial.

The follow-through

Because follow-through is so important, be sure to pick time frames and consequences that will be easy for you to stick with. One family might think a month is no big deal, and another might think a week is more comfortable.

Once it is set up, let it go! No nagging. No reminders. Let them figure it out. Part of the initial follow-through is doing what you said you would do. In this example, it was to leave them alone. The expectations and consequences have been set; let them happen on their own. Let them feel the consequences of possibly messing up and the pleasure of success. If you meddle, it will be about you, rather than about their growth. Show them you have hope in them by leaving it alone.

If the behavior does not change and you must implement the agreed-upon consequences, do not use language that states disappointment or anger. Apply the consequences calmly and consistently. Without judgment, ask your teen what they think went wrong. Review the parameters and start again.

Setting new boundaries

As the parent starts to learn about healthy parenting, changes will happen, and new boundaries will be established. Changing all the boundaries at once is too much. Pick a few that address safety issues first. Then work on the ones that will bring more harmony to the house. Some examples can be:

- If anyone yells, including the parents, they must take a walk around the block to cool off.

- Wednesday will be family dinner night.
- There will no longer be any electronics at mealtimes.
- Everyone will take a turn cooking a dinner.

Boundaries and house rules bring structure and clarity to household expectations. The adults in the house need to all agree to the boundaries and stick to them. If one adult in the house says, "No computer before dinner." and the other adult is saying, "Go play video games while I make dinner." then you are not helping your teen. Consistency builds trust and safety. We know we have said this before, but when setting new boundaries, you need to be clear and specific and let them know the consequences.

TRY THIS
CHECK IN

WHEN WAS THE LAST TIME YOU ENGAGED YOUR TEEN IN A CONVERSATION WHERE YOU HAD NO OBJECTIVE? THAT MEANS YOU SAT DOWN JUST TO SAY, "HEY," AND LISTEN TO HOW THEY ARE DOING. YOU AREN'T LOOKING FOR INFORMATION, YOU AREN'T CORRECTING SOMETHING, AND YOU AREN'T TELLING THEM YOUR STORY. TRY APPROACHING YOUR TEEN WITH THE SOLE PURPOSE OF LISTENING TO THEM. DO NOT TRY TO FIX ANY PROBLEMS, GIVE THEM INFORMATION, OR GET INFORMATION—JUST LISTEN.

THRIVE and Talking with Your Teen

Trust—Trust that your teen wants a relationship with you based on open and honest communication.

Heal—Modifying how you communicate and problem solve issues, can heal your relationship with your teen.

Respect—Choose your time and place carefully when seeking out a conversation with your teen. Show them respect and model how you want them to communicate.

Invite—Invite your teen into a collaborative conversation with you.

Validate—Validating your teen's emotions and reactions before apologizing, can be very powerful for keeping the dialogue going.

Enjoy—Use humor, but remember, never at the expense of your teen.

Chapter 6

THE TEEN BRAIN

"Around the age of thirteen, kids' brains shift from focusing on their mothers' voices to favor new voices, part of the biological signal driving teens to separate from their parents, a Stanford Medicine study has found" (Digitale, 2022). That's right! Just as you suspected! The teen brain is turning them against you…well, sort of. Studies show that in early childhood, the child brain stimulates their reward center when they hear mom. Around the age of thirteen, their brain starts giving them more pleasure when they hear new voices. This emphasizes that they are changing, and it's not about you when they start pulling away. It is a part of the growing-up process.

This is one example of the many things happening inside your teen's body. Their brain alone has so much going on during this time.

The Individuation Process

As mentioned above, their brain is pulling away, and they are designed to start exploring outside the family for adulthood. This is called *individuation*. *Individuating* is a big psychology word that means they are becoming an adult and need to figure out who they are, independent of the family. If this is done in a healthy way, they will eventually interact with you as an adult in a loving way—you just might have to wait a few years for it. The stepping away from the family allows them to ask, "Is everything I learned in my childhood really mine?" This question can only be answered by them. The more parents insist on inserting themselves in answering this big question, the more likely their teen will rebel.

At the same time, they are trying to make big choices and figure out who they are, and yet the part of their brain that is best at making big decisions is not fully developed. "The rational part of a teen's brain isn't fully developed and won't be until age twenty-five or so" (Stanford Children's Health, 2022). This cannot be news to any parent or guardian. They watch their teen act impulsively and do things that often make no sense. It can get worse when they get into groups. The mob brain takes over. So what is a parent to do?

Your teen does need you. They need your guidance, approval, acceptance, and support. When they do something that doesn't really make sense, give them time to learn from what they did. Ask them questions and encourage them to think about what has happened. Talk with them about consequences, both positive and negative. This is where the family dinner becomes crucial. Ask about their day in specific ways, "Any big challenges today? How did you handle it?"

When asking about their day, remember that if they are struggling with something, don't jump to fix it. Teaching them to problem solve means letting them practice problem solving. Some good follow up questions might be:

- How do you want to handle this issue?
- What do you think are some of the possible outcomes to this issue?
- What do you have control over in this situation?
- Do you need anything from me in this situation?
- What "what ifs…" have you considered? (If they only have negative "what ifs…" remind them to try on a few positive ones.)

The fact is their brain is not going to process the world the same way you do. You may be seeing them as impulsive and reckless. Conversely, they may see your adult thoughts as boring and overcautious. Just as you would hate for them to say, "Why are you so controlling?" the same is true when you say to them, "Why are you being so reckless?"

There's a reason for their brain to be this way. Think about it. They are at an age where they need to be bold and passionate. They are leaving the nest, starting to develop intimate relationships, acting independent for the first time, etc. The same downside that causes them to be rash also helps them to be brave. While parents often think everything through, the teen is jumping in and taking chances. Learning to celebrate this season of their life can be exciting. Instead of fighting the way they think, try offering guidance.

TRY THIS
ELIMINATE "WHY?"

WHEN ASKING YOUR TEEN QUESTIONS, TRY TO ELIMINATE "WHY?" OF THE POSSIBLE CHOICES, IT IS THE QUESTION THAT SOUNDS MOST JUDGMENTAL AND RARELY LEADS TO ANY TYPE OF OPEN DISCUSSION. OBSERVE YOUR USE OF THE WORD "WHY" FOR ONE WEEK. IF POSSIBLE, SEE HOW LONG YOU CAN GO WITHOUT ASKING "WHY?" FOR A MORE ADVANCED TASK, TRY THIS WITH EVERYONE IN YOUR LIFE, EVEN WITH FRIENDS AND COLLEAGUES. HERE ARE SOME ALTERNATIVES:

- HMM...TELL ME MORE ABOUT THAT.
- WHAT HAPPENED NEXT?
- HOW DID YOU HANDLE IT?
- WHAT DID YOU DO?
- HOW DO YOU FEEL ABOUT THE WAY THAT TURNED OUT?

CURIOSITY CAN BE VERY POWERFUL WHEN IT ISN'T DRENCHED IN JUDGMENT.

In 2020, our children and teens experienced a cautious world, and we can't imagine yet how it will impact the thinking of future generations. We are also dealing with teens who have spent their whole lives with the digital world all around them. A consequence to this is that many teens now refrain from being physically active and adventurous. Instead, channeling this physical energy into a virtual reality using avatars to represent them. Caution and physical isolation are becoming more commonplace.

Self-esteem

If you are not guiding them, but just speaking at them (or yelling), they will very quickly turn to external influences. No one is attracted to people who criticize them and are often angry with them. It is already in their nature at this age to seek out these outside voices, so how can you be a part of that? Holding on too tightly will only create a battle of wills. Conversely, not participating will create an unsafe environment for your teen. What does collaboration and healthy self-esteem look like?

Building up your teen's self-esteem may be the best tool for fighting other people's negative influences. Teens with a high self-esteem are more likely to make positive choices in their lives. Encouraging self-esteem at home is about respect and communication. It is helping your teen to think critically about social media and the Internet, setting goals they must work for and then feeling the satisfaction of achievement, and developing close, healthy friendships.

They will have a natural dip in their self-esteem as they transition from childhood to the teen years because they are tired of being treated "like a kid" (Pickhardt, 2010). What a great opportunity for the parent. They need you to give them new responsibilities and freedoms as they move out of childhood and toward adulthood. Have a discussion with your teen about new expectations and the freedoms they can begin to explore independently. They need to know that you feel they are capable. Give them opportunities to try new experiences with your support.

As your teen is experiencing new ways to interact with the outside world, they will rely on the calm, clear, and consistent boundaries at home to feel safe. If you have ever watched a toddler at the park, they walk away from their parent seeking adventure, then eventually they come back to check in with their safety, and then they are off again. Teens are no different in that they are seeking newness and adventure, but they also need to know they are safe (although they will be the last to admit it). This whole process of independently exploring knowing they are supported by a safe environment will build their self-esteem.

Mental Health Issues

The teen years see a lot of firsts. Unfortunately, some firsts that happen often are depression, anxiety, and anger management issues. These are prime years for these mental health issues to show up in people's lives. Here we will give you a few things to look for and when to call a therapist. Not all symptoms need to be present for you to seek help. Anything you feel may be distressing for your teen can be reason enough. If the symptoms are interfering with their regular day-to-day life, then it is time to consult with a mental health professional.

Understanding the symptoms

The following list of symptoms provided for depression and anxiety are referenced from the DSM-5-TR (American Psychiatric Association, 2022).

Depression

Be aware that signs of depression can be situational, which means that the symptoms may come and go depending on life circumstances. This type of depression should not be cause for alarm. But when symptoms are present and persistent for two or more weeks, it may be time to intervene. The general symptoms of depression include:

- Depressed or irritable mood most of the day (sad, empty, hopeless, numb)
- Loss in pleasure in doing things that were previously enjoyed
- Change in appetite and/or rapid weight loss or gain
- Trouble sleeping or oversleeping (teens need about eight to nine hours of sleep)
- Fatigue or loss of energy
- Low self-esteem and excessive negative thinking
- Brain fog, lack of concentration, and indecisiveness
- Recurrent thoughts of death (if your teen is suicidal and seems to have a plan call 911)
- Be aware if these symptoms are linked to their menstrual cycle

Anxiety

Anxiety can be in many forms as well. Teens may suffer with symptoms related to specific phobias, social anxiety, and/or experiencing panic attacks for the first time. They may not realize they can learn tools to manage this. The general symptoms of anxiety include:

- Excessive worry on more days than not
- Trouble controlling the worry
- Restlessness or on edge
- Fatigue
- Difficulty concentrating and going blank
- Irritability
- Muscle tension
- Sleep disturbance

Anger management issues

Anger heavily impacts males in the late teen years due to a surge in testosterone. If your teen is out of control in their anger, a therapist can teach them skills on how to express their feelings in productive ways. The therapist can also help a family, as a whole, learn skills to manage family arguments, develop communication skills, and set healthy boundaries.

TRY THIS
INVESTIGATE THE PROBLEM

1. MAKE A LIST OF ALL THE SYMPTOMS YOU ARE SEEING IN YOUR TEEN. IF THERE ARE ANY PHYSICAL PROBLEMS LIKE WEIGHT CHANGE, LOSS OF APPETITE, OR SLEEP ISSUES, HIGHLIGHT THOSE AS IMPORTANT.

2. BE SURE TO START BY VISITING YOUR TEEN'S DOCTOR FOR A CHECKUP TO RULE OUT ANY POSSIBLE MEDICAL PROBLEMS. MENTION THE SYMPTOMS THAT ARE CAUSING CONCERN.

3. MAKE A SEPARATE LIST OF ALL THE WAYS IT IS AFFECTING THE FAMILY. THINK OF POSSIBLE GOALS THAT THERAPY MIGHT HELP WITH. SOME EXAMPLES MIGHT BE:

   - BUILD FAMILY COMMUNICATION
   - SKILL BUILDING IN DEALING WITH DEPRESSION, ANXIETY, OR BEREAVEMENT
   - REDUCING FAMILY ARGUMENTS
   - UNDERSTANDING FAMILY BOUNDARIES
   - HEALING BROKEN FAMILY RELATIONSHIPS

4. BE SURE TO COLLABORATE WITH YOUR TEEN IN THIS PROCESS. DON'T MAKE THEM FEEL LIKE THERAPY IS A PUNISHMENT FOR "BAD BEHAVIOR." THIS WILL ONLY BUILD RESISTANCE.

5. FINALLY, CHOOSE A THERAPIST.

Individual or family therapy

Most first sessions in teenage therapy involve the parent or guardian. The family will be asked simply, "What brought you in today?" The first session is a time for you to understand the therapist's style and expectations. The therapist should help you decide what kind of therapy is best for your family. But here are a few pointers to help with your expectations.

Individual therapy is appropriate if the teen is struggling with something painful at school, is depressed, angry, anxious, grieving the loss of someone or something, or wants to talk about something freely without their parents listening in (some of them have never had the freedom to have a private space to really share about their struggles). The therapist should explain the levels of confidentiality they keep when working with your teen. Even though your teen is in individual therapy, you can expect updates and may even be invited to a session for skill building or for your teen to share what is going on in their life. Parents may also be given parenting tips specific to supporting the teen in this process. Some parents have never experienced depression or anxiety and struggle to help their child. A therapist can become a great ally in getting tools to help their teen.

Family therapy is appropriate when there is a change in the family dynamics and/or communication within the family begins to break down, impacting your teen's behaviors. Family therapy may include all members of the household or only the individuals directly impacted by the situation. It's important to remember that therapy isn't about fixing a broken person but helping people manage their challenging world.

We've talked about how life can throw curve balls at us, and it's okay to ask for help. Therapy is not a permanent commitment. You can try it out, and if it doesn't fit, it's okay to either find a different therapist or do something different. Giving it three or four sessions is usually enough to know if this is a useful tool.

Highlighted Concepts

Here are some concepts about the brain and psychology, which might help you better understand yourself and your teen.

Reversing negative self-talk

Many teens have a tendency toward negative self-talk (Don't we all?). This happens when feelings and thoughts get muddled. Even adults struggle to properly label their thoughts and feelings. We often make the mistake of thinking our feelings and thoughts are the same. Feelings are a true reaction to a situation that just occurred. Feelings are simply information, no more, no less. Thoughts are what we decide or how we judge those feelings, which can take the information and change what the feeling is trying to tell us. If we mislabel our feelings, we can cause bigger and more negative feelings, but we can also help move our feelings toward healing and positivity. It's all about learning our thinking patterns.

For example, if your teen's partner breaks up with them, their initial feeling may be loss or sadness. This is an appropriate feeling for the situation. The information the feeling is giving your teen is that they just lost someone who was important to them. As parents, we should provide support (even if you are secretly happy they broke up). However, if they take this feeling of sadness and think to themselves that the partner broke up with them because, "I am not good enough," then this thought changes the appropriate initial feeling of loss to a dysfunctional feeling of self-loathing or disgust. These feelings and thoughts have very different mental health outcomes.

Try making a statement about a challenging situation and how you are feeling about it. Many people think they are talking about their feelings but are actually using their thoughts to describe what they are "feeling." "I feel like I failed" is a thought, not a feeling. It combines "I feel disappointed, and I think I'm a failure." Clarifying your thoughts and emotions can help you have more power over your negative self-talk. The best trick to decipher the different between a thought and a feeling is to say, "I feel ___________." A feeling is one word; a thought is a full sentence. If you can master this, teach this skill to your teen.

The feeling wheel is a great tool for teaching your teen on how to clearly identify their feelings, which can make a huge impact on their mental health. Parents should be cautious to not identify their teens feelings for them. Try to avoid questions like "Why are you sad?" This assumes a feeling before they have named it.

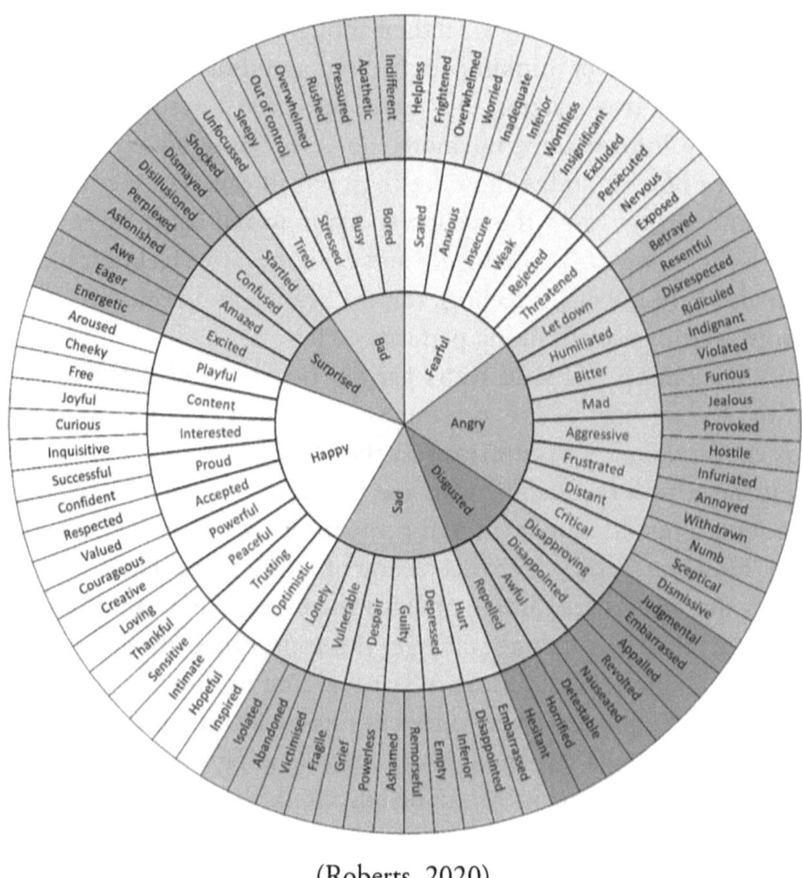

(Roberts, 2020)

Once the feeling is labeled, identify the thoughts connected to that specific feeling. In doing this, we have an opportunity to challenge or reframe this thought. This is an important step as it may impact the actions we take. Parents will want to examine the thought to ensure it isn't being made through a distorted filter. Here are some common distortions (also referred to in psychology as cognitive distortions or thinking errors):

- Thinking one situation will define all other situations
- Predicting what people are thinking or going to say (humans are terrible mind readers!)
- Highlighting only negative comments and ignoring anything good
- Believing you "have to" because "they" said so, but not knowing who "they" are
- Catastrophizing (that's a fun word for blowing it out of proportion)

Once the truth is identified, it is easier to challenge the thought process. For example, a teen might tell themselves, "They won't like me, so I'm not even going to try to be their friend." This thought process is combining the cognitive distortions of mind reading and catastrophizing. If we change the thought to exclude the distortions, a teen might tell themselves, "I can't know what other people think, so I will ask them to hang out." Modifying these thoughts will directly impact the actions they take.

Fixed vs. open mindset

Fixed mindset and open mindset are becoming popular buzz words among teachers and people in the world of psychology (Dweck, 2006). Probably the best way to explain it is to give an example. If a teen gets a poor grade on a test, you can tell what kind of mindset they have based on their reaction. If they say, "Well I was never good at that subject," they might have a fixed mindset. They see their knowledge of that topic as fixed. If they say, "I guess I will have to study harder or differently before the next test." This teen has an open mindset. They take responsibility for their situation and see the impact their choices have on affecting the future.

Having an open mindset is ideal. As a parent, you can impact your teen's way of thinking by making small changes to language. When a negative thought is expressed by your teen, try adding words like "for now," "yet," or something of that nature to imply possible change.

- I can't seem to understand my math homework…yet.
- I feel like everything I do is wrong…for now.
- I don't know what I want to be when I graduate…at this moment.
- Why can't I get a job…right now?
- No one wants to date me…so far.

Help them to recognize absolute statements are limiting and highlight that circumstances are time limited. This will present opportunities for your teen to look at situation through a temporary and flexible lens. This open mindset presents the opportunity for critical thinking.

Having an open mindset might not come naturally to your teen. Don't shame them for not thinking openly. Give them tools to make small changes toward having a more productive look at their circumstances. Rephrase statements they make that are fixed, with open statements but still showing you hear them.

- I bombed that test. I'm never going to understand biology.
    - I know it's frustrating that you didn't do well on that test. It must feel like you will never get it, at least for now. Do you need help with studying?
- All my friends hate me. I'm never going to fit in.
    - I know the fight you had with your friends makes it feel like that right now. High school friendships often go through a lot of transitions. It can be hard to connect sometimes.

These statements aren't going to fix things instantly. Teens are supposed to go through some struggles to grow. These are just to help them shift their thinking as they problem solve. They need validation in their frustration, but then you offer them hope, by helping them see it is not a permanent situation. You help them shift into the open mindset.

TRY THIS
JOURNAL THOUGHTS AND FEELINGS

JOURNAL THOUGHTS AND FEELINGS TO INCREASE YOUR AWARENESS OF HOW YOU INTERPRET YOUR REACTIONS TO SITUATIONS WITH YOUR TEEN. IF YOU ARE NOTICING NEGATIVE WORDS LIKE DEFEATED, STUPID, AND NEVER, ASK YOURSELF IF YOU CAN CHANGE THE WORDS YOU USE TO DESCRIBE YOUR FEELINGS TO BE MORE CONSTRUCTIVE.

Introvert vs. extrovert

People often confuse introvert with "shy" and extrovert with "outgoing." The problem with that is that shyness is not permanent and being outgoing can be taught. Shyness and outgoingness are behaviors. Everyone has times in their life when they need to be alone and other times when they need to be around their friends. Introversion and extraversion are personality characteristics that are on a continuum and can vary from one extreme to another. Introversion and extroversion are a hard-wired part of each person's brain that define how they recharge their energy and connect with others.

Extroverts

Being an extrovert means that your teen charges their "battery" up by being around people. The extrovert will feel a wave of energy from a sense of connecting with others. Even accomplishing chores around the house can be more fun for the extrovert if they have someone nearby. A shy extrovert could be struggling. If your teen charges up by being around people but has social anxiety or a fear of reaching out, they may become low on energy and even get depressed.

Connecting with people is a skill; so is being a good friend. If you have a teen who struggles to connect, you may want to take some time to help them brainstorm ways to develop their community. Talk about taking a chance and inviting people over. Process when friendships fall apart. Friendships change a lot during the teen years.

Your extrovert is more likely an external processor. Hearing all their thoughts can be daunting if you tend toward jumping to conclusions. Give them time to speak and even go back on what they are saying. Their current statement could be a thought that is still developing and may not be their final opinion.

Introverts

Your introvert may love a good party, but eventually it may drain them. They recharge by having alone time. A parent can misinterpret their introverted teen as unhappy when they are simply enjoying some solo time. This is when knowing your teen and how they process can be important. Knowing the difference between an introvert who needs downtime and a depressed individual can be crucial to how you interact with your teen.

Introverts enjoy close friendships who understand their need to also be alone. When an introverted person spends time with others, all of their energy goes to trying to understand and connect with those other people, leaving no energy for themselves. An introvert needs to have time to recharge so that connections with others are possible. The difference between a depressed teen and an introvert is that after a time of solitude, the introvert will reach out and still maintain connections with their friends.

Extrovert vs. introvert brains

The introvert brain is physically different than the extrovert brain. Dopamine is produced in both brains, but the extrovert is less sensitive to it and can need more of it. The introvert will become overwhelmed by an excess of dopamine (Charles, n.d.). The pathways to each of the decision-making parts of their brains are different as well. The extrovert can make quick decisions versus the introvert, whose thoughts need to travel through more gray matter. Introverts may take longer to make a choice, but they will more likely stand by their choice over time.

Celebrating these differences is a wonderful gift to your teen. Don't try to fit your teen into the mold that matches your thinking. Help them be proud of their uniqueness if they are the only introvert or extrovert in the family. You can also help them normalize that there are many great thinkers in both the introvert and extrovert world.

Most importantly they are going to think differently than you for so many reasons. Honor that and be prepared to make an effort to understand their point of view. You don't have to agree with them, but at least, show them respect in listening to their ideas and thoughts.

TRY THIS
ONE-ON-ONE TIME

IF YOU HAVE MORE THAN ONE CHILD, PLAN A NIGHT WITH JUST ONE OF THEM. KEEP IN MIND THEIR PERSONALITY. YOU CAN'T REALLY GO WRONG WITH GOING OUT FOR DINNER OR DESSERT. KEEP IT SIMPLE OR GLAM IT UP. IT DOESN'T MATTER. THE POINT IS TO FOCUS ON YOUR TEEN. IF THEY ARE AN EXTROVERT, REMEMBER TO LET THEM HAVE THOUGHTS OUT LOUD. IF THEY ARE INTROVERTS, GIVE THEM TIME TO ANSWER QUESTIONS. DON'T TALK OVER THEM. IF THERE IS A LULL IN THE CONVERSATION, MAYBE SHARE A STORY FROM YOUR TEEN YEARS THAT THEY HAVE NEVER HEARD.

The Internet and the Brain

The Internet has a lot of great resources and can be a powerful tool for learning. In addition, "seven systematic reviews published to date have found an association between increased screen time and worse mental health in young people" (Sedgwick, Epstein, Dutta, & Ougrin, 2019). The Internet has put today's teen on display since they were born. With posts about gender reveals, birthdays, first day of school, "promposals," and every cute thing they do, it's not surprising they let the Internet dictate how they feel about themselves. It's no wonder that they are aware of acceptance through social media.

Social media

Being a teen is an awkward time. They already have the world watching them through Internet posts from everyone they know including themselves. They are aware of being friended, unfriended, liked, and not liked by being ignored. They compare their posts to other people's posts all the time. Often their value is very much tied into social media. Due to this, airing your teen's mistakes or behavior online may impact how they view and feel about themselves. To hash out family issues publicly for everyone to read can be humiliating.

There are *influencers* that put their lives online, and today's teens sometimes make the mistake of thinking that they are seeing the whole story. It's easy for anyone to get sucked into someone's online story and forget that it is only a minute or two of their day or week. Today's teens get lost in thoughts comparing themselves to a fantasy. Teens can be overwhelmed with negative self-talk because they think they know these people online, whom they have never met, and wish their lives were more like theirs.

As mentioned earlier, your teen is looking for people to inspire them during these years. It might be your job to help them find healthy options outside the nuclear family (and maybe even offline). In the "olden days," teens would take on apprenticeships and learn a trade. The master tradespeople would mentor them and teach them a skill. Currently, teens are influenced by online people that care more about how many followers they have than your teen and their needs. They are sometimes people with twisted intentions who could be causing your teen great harm.

Without critical thinking skills about social media, your teen could be in danger of broken self-esteem, suicidal ideation, self-harm, depression, anxiety, etc. As mentioned before, the teen brain is seeking outside influences. What voices are they listening to? How are you helping them make good choices? Both rigid restrictions and complete freedom on the Internet are ignoring the issue. This is where using your skills in communication and SMART goal setting can help develop healthy Internet use.

TRY THIS
SOCIAL MEDIA AND THE FULL STORY

Open up your phone and scroll through the pictures. Ask yourself and your teen the following: If an outsider saw these pictures, what story would they see about your family? Would they see the family struggles or happy vacation pictures? Can someone really know your family from these pictures? Develop some critical thinking around social media posts. Then pull up some influencer posts. Explore some parts of the story that may be missing.

- Do we know how they resolve issues?
- Do we know their relationship with the whole family?
- Do we know what they are struggling with? Doesn't everyone have something they are struggling with?
- Could they be using a filter? (You might try some of the filters—they are amazing.)
- Do we know what makes them laugh? Cry? Get angry?

Are digital relationships enough?

Digital relationships have become the norm in this digital age and especially in the wake of lockdowns. It was great for teens to chat with friends and keep relationships when students were isolated by a pandemic. As the dust settles, it may be important to ask, is it enough for authentic connection? Can we even thrive socially online? "Apart from the addictive nature of our new digital way of connecting, does not seem to satisfy our deep-seeded need for true human contact. Instead, what it seems to have spawned is the illusion of social connection" (Kardaras, 2020). Encouraging your teen to step away from the computer and develop friendships at school and in the neighborhood will help build a stronger self-esteem and enable better social health and genuine connections with others.

Porn and the brain

The topic of pornography is probably a topic that parents are uncomfortable with and may even be tempted to skip reading about. Not taking it seriously can be a big mistake. The Internet porn of today is not the porn mags of old. With high levels of availability, fast access to stranger and darker video clips, and an industry that is hoping to capture the mind of young teens, it is becoming a real problem. "The age of first viewing has continued to drop, with 69% of males and 23% of females first viewing porn at age thirteen or younger" (Wilson, 2017).

Imagine your teen is spiraling down a path of video clips filled with sexual behaviors that make them feel both embarrassed and fascinated. They might start questioning why they are drawn to video clips that they would be embarrassed to talk about with even their friends. The level of shame is high and causes so much pain. With addiction comes hiding the evidence and lying to loved ones to cover the shame.

Studies show it is rewiring their brains. "JAMA psychiatry published research showing that, even in moderate porn users, use correlates with reduced grey matter and decreased sexual responsiveness"

(Wilson, 2017). Teens exposed to such graphic images, before they start dating, develop social anxiety and depression, impacting their abilities to form in-person relationships.

Masturbating to pornography changes how our brains connect sex to physical pleasure. Depending on the type of pornography being viewed will determine the direction in which the addiction intensifies. Education on the effects of Internet pornography and the teenage brain allows for an open discussion, eliminating the stigma and embarrassment related to sexuality and pornography.

As the parent, you can't be everywhere the Internet is. Help them be aware of the possible dangers. Have open conversations about the Internet, porn, and addiction. Teens are not deviant in this behavior, but can become victims of the predator, known as Internet porn.

THRIVE and the Teen Brain

Trust—Trust they are not rejecting you for personal reasons. It's what they are designed to do. It's biology.

Heal—Be patient during the teen years as they go through many changes and assist them in healing if they have a broken self-esteem.

Respect—Respect that their brain works differently than yours.

Invite—Invite them into open and nonjudgmental conversations about their Internet use.

Validate—Validate their need for voices outside the family. Help them find healthy mentors.

Enjoy—Enjoy their passion for the things they are interested in. Celebrate and share in their boldness.

Chapter 7

NOT JUST A BODY

If there is one thing that wreaks havoc on the teen self-esteem more than anything, it is their bodies. Puberty is not a gentle process. One sixteen-year-old male teen can look like a twenty-five-year-old man with a beard, and his best friend of the same age can look like a twelve-year-old boy. The same is true for females. One can look like a fully developed woman and the other like a little girl. With new gender definitions, which are popular with teens, it gets even more complicated. Social media increases the comparison as teens are constantly bombarded with images and influencers, impacting how they feel about themselves. The teen body is almost guaranteed to betray them in some way.

Let's dig a little deeper into this body betrayal. We talked about the identity phase of development, and now you understand that your teen is trying to figure themselves out. Part of that process is comparison. Body comparison can be brutal and cruel, especially if they are comparing themselves to the "Hollywood teen" (Are they even teenagers?). There are so many social media platforms that depend on "likes" and people commenting "You look so good." If they don't get the same amount of reaction as others, they sometimes question their own looks and value.

When teens compare themselves to their friends and peers, they don't see the whole picture. Everyone is struggling with something, but your teen is probably not thinking about other people's struggles. When they see each other, they often only see what their friends have that they don't. For example, "Emma is so pretty. She has a perfect body. I wish I looked like her. She's so lucky. Of course, she has the best boyfriend. He's so hot." Meanwhile Emma is struggling with anxiety, wishes she could get her parents to stop fighting, and feels pressured by her boyfriend to have sex when she doesn't feel ready. No teen's life is perfect.

TRY THIS
IS THAT A TEEN?

WORK ON THIS ONE WITH YOUR TEEN. LIST ALL THE TEENS YOU KNOW FROM TELEVISION AND MOVIES. LOOK UP THE ACTORS' AGES AND SEE WHAT AGE THEY REALLY ARE. CAN YOU GUESS BEFORE LOOKING IF THEY ARE A TEEN OR AN ADULT? DISCUSS WHAT IT IS LIKE TO SEE ADULTS PLAYING TEENAGERS.

Teens have acne, braces, boobs (or no boobs), cracking voices, menstruation, involuntary erections, growing pains, body hair (wanted or unwanted), weight gain or loss, etc. That's just the everyday stuff. If they have learning disorders, anxiety, depression, or illness, it becomes overwhelming, and they can become convinced they have no value. Be cautious when commenting on your teen's body because they are already hard enough on themselves.

Teens put a lot of pressure on themselves to look a certain way. Flaws are focused on and highlighted in their minds. Young teens are reportedly taking filtered pictures of themselves to the plastic surgeon asking to look like the filter made them look. Their sense of self can easily become distorted if not given some guidance. So how do you, the adult in their life, help them to take stock of the whole self and accept who they are? How do you connect with them at a different place so they have better self-esteem and you can deepen your relationship with them?

Acceptance

There is not a one-size-fits-all for acceptance. We will explore different areas that you can encourage your teen. This is because we are trying to develop the whole person. Developing balance in all aspects of their life will help them build a stronger self-esteem. Looks are important to your teen; therefore, they are important to discuss. However, looks are only skin deep. Character building is a big part of transitioning from childhood to adulthood.

Modeling healthy behavior

We have discussed how being a positive role model to your teen is a very powerful way of showing them healthy ways of living. You may not realize what language you are using to talk about your own body or who you are as a whole person. Here are some questions to help you consider how you might be presenting yourself to your teen:

- Do you use negative words to describe your body?
- Do you love yourself and value who you are as a person?
- Does vanity take a higher place in your life over what kind of person you are?
- How do you talk about food and exercise?
- Are you kind or critical?

Think about how you want your teen to think about themselves. Model and encourage healthy choices. Talk about the character of a person and how to develop it.

> ## TRY THIS
> ## MY FAVORITE PEOPLE
>
> HERE IS AN EXERCISE YOU CAN DO WITH YOUR TEEN.
>
> 1. MAKE A LIST OF THE THREE PEOPLE IN YOUR LIFE WHOM YOU LOVE MOST.
> 2. LIST THREE THINGS THAT YOU LOVE ABOUT THEM.
> 3. LIST THREE THINGS THAT MAKE YOU FEEL LOVED BY THEM.
>
> NOW EXPLORE THE WORDS USED TO DESCRIBE THE CONNECTION. DID YOU USE WORDS LIKE "THEY ARE SO GORGEOUS"? IS VANITY SOMETHING THAT CONNECTS YOU TO OTHERS? MOST DON'T DESCRIBE THEIR FAVORITE PEOPLE AS SUPERMODEL PERFECT. WHAT OTHER WORDS WERE USED? KIND? GENEROUS? FUNNY? LOVING? PICK ONE OF THE CHARACTERISTICS YOU LISTED AND THINK OF ONE THING YOU CAN DO THIS WEEK TO DEVELOP THAT CHARACTERISTIC IN YOURSELF.
>
> *NOTE: SOMETHING TO CONSIDER. WE ALL KNOW ATTRACTIVE PEOPLE WHO, ONCE THEY SPEAK, ARE RUDE OR UNKIND. WE ALSO KNOW PEOPLE WHO MIGHT BE DESCRIBED AS "PLAIN" BUT HAVE QUALITIES LIKE KINDNESS OR A GOOD SENSE OF HUMOR THAT CONNECT US TO THEM. SOMETIMES THAT CONNECTION HELPS US TO SEE THEM AS BEAUTIFUL. HOW DO YOU WANT TO BE THOUGHT OF?

Building self-esteem through relationship

A big part of self-esteem for your teen is based in the relationship you have with them. If you accept them and show them love, then they will feel lovable. Teens need regular affection and connection. Some teens may set boundaries around hugging (especially in front of their friends). It's okay to let them set those boundaries. It's not personal. Show affection in different ways, like offering to drive them and their friends.

Try to enjoy them. Harsh words, constant criticism, and rejection are just bullying. Many people can hear ten positive things and one criticism, and that criticism will stick with them. As parents, you have an opportunity to lift up your teen and make them feel good about themselves. A caution is to not use false praise. Making sure you are genuine about your affection will help them feel it. Teens have an amazing radar for dishonesty. They are often skeptical already, so being sincere will go a long way.

When you spend time with them, point out their strengths. Be sure to be specific. "You're so smart" or "I'm proud of you" doesn't tell them the whole story and can easily be set aside. "I love how hard you have been working on your homework lately. It shows a lot of grit. I know it's been challenging," or "I am so proud of how you have been treating your little sibling lately. I know they can be tiring for you at times, but you have been really stepping up and being kind. Thank you."

Schedule quality time to spend with your teen doing something you both enjoy. Show them you value their company. When you do, don't attach any strings. Sometimes parents overdo the teaching moments. Just hanging out together can be a simple yet powerful message of acceptance.

Friendships are another kind of relationship that can influence your teen's self-acceptance. If they don't have close friends, it would be important to give them the skills to connect more deeply with their peers. It is never too late to make new friends. Maintaining a friendship is something that can be taught. If your teen struggles in this area, teach them how to be curious, empathetic, and intentional with other people. If they only have one or two true friends that they connect with, don't panic. That's plenty for most people, especially your introvert.

Make sure they understand that high school friendships can sometimes change as people go through their own life changes. A new significant other, a move, and a new student at school can all make a huge impact on a friend group. Teach your teen to not take these changes personally. Some teens will think there is something wrong with them when they are between friends. Being between friend groups does not mean they have a problem; they are just in the process of rebuilding their circle.

Fitness

With regard to mental health, it is often said, "If you aren't exercising, eating right, and sleeping well, then you are not even trying to fight your depression, anxiety." Fitness increases the feel-good chemicals in your brain, improves sleep, allows time to think and process your day, and improves your feelings of achievement as you set and meet goals.

We understand that motivation is one of the things your teen may struggle with. Being a cheerleader for your kids can be an important part of their fitness. They may lack the motivation to get started. Offer to do an activity with them. Maybe issue a challenge with a reward. Maybe sign up for something fun (they have themed 5K runs, dance classes, or team sports). Pick activities they like.

TRY THIS
FAMILY FUN TOURNAMENT

CREATE A LIST OF CHALLENGES YOU CAN DO AS A FAMILY. BE CREATIVE AND GO BEYOND JUST PHYSICAL CHALLENGES. BE SURE TO INCLUDE THINGS YOUR TEEN IS GREAT AT. SOME EXAMPLES:

- SHOOT HOOPS IN THE LOCAL SCHOOLYARD.
- BALANCE A BOOK ON YOUR HEAD.
- CREATE A CLASSIC ART PIECE (*STARRY NIGHT* BY VAN GOGH IS FUN).
- TONGUE TWISTERS.
- CREATE AN OBSTACLE COURSE IN THE HOUSE.

BE CREATIVE! THIS CAN BE DONE OVER A FEW DAYS, AN AFTERNOON, OR WHATEVER WORKS FOR YOUR FAMILY. CREATE PRIZES THAT EVERYONE WILL ENJOY. IF YOU HAVE A TEEN WHO STRUGGLES WITH LOSING, USE THIS OPPORTUNITY TO TEACH THEM HOW TO LOSE WITH GRACE (MODEL IT).

Sleep

Sleep can be a powerful healer. "Teens need nine to nine and a half hours of sleep per night—that's an hour or so more than they needed at age ten… Additional sleep supports their developing brain, as well as physical growth spurts. It also helps protect them from serious consequences like depression or drug use" (Johns Hopkins Medicine, 2021). How does sleep bring balance to their self-esteem? Having the right amount of sleep will help them approach their challenges with a rested mind.

Making sure your teen has good sleep hygiene can be a challenge. You might be asking, "What is sleep hygiene?" It is the routines, the setting in the bedroom, and all the other aspects of good sleep. Here are some basics that can be crucial to a good night's sleep:

- Consistent bedtimes and bedtime routines.
- Turning off electronics at night (we'd say an hour before, but we know that may be a lot harder).
- Control the light in the room (a good sleep mask can go a long way).
- Some people like white noise (calm music, fan noise…)

Pick one to work on. Giving your teen a huge list of changes is often overwhelming. If they are struggling with bad sleep, give them a couple of options to try and have them pick one they think they can comfortably try.

Many people, especially teens, will find that if they have anxiety or depression, bedtime can be very difficult. Journaling, prayer, or meditating on a specific word before bed can be very powerful. If you are the last to talk to them at the end of the day, leave them with a positive statement.

TRY THIS
FIVE SENSES

(GREAT FOR PANIC ATTACKS OR NIGHTTIME RUMINATIONS)

BE VERY SPECIFIC ABOUT COUNTING IN THIS EXERCISE. USING NUMBERS AND COMING UP WITH ANSWERS KEEPS BOTH SIDES OF YOUR BRAIN OCCUPIED.

- NAME FIVE THINGS YOU SEE.
- NAME FOUR THINGS YOU CAN TOUCH.
- NAME THREE THINGS YOU CAN HEAR.
- NAME TWO THINGS YOU CAN SMELL.
- WHAT DOES YOUR MOUTH TASTE LIKE?

Here is another fun activity to keep the brain occupied when nighttime overthinking gets in the way of sleep:

> ### TRY THIS
> ### CATEGORIES
>
> SOMETIMES OUR BRAINS GO INTO HYPERDRIVE IN THE MIDDLE OF THE NIGHT. USING THE ALPHABET, LIST THINGS IN ONE CATEGORY TO DISTRACT YOURSELF FROM YOUR THOUGHTS. FOR EXAMPLE:
>
> - BABY NAMES
>   - ALLEN, BEATRICE, CARMEN…
> - FOODS
>   - APPLE, BENTO BOX, CANDY…
> - PLACES YOU HAVE VISITED
>   - ART STUDIO, BANK, CANADA…
>
> BE CREATIVE WITH YOUR CATEGORY. IT'S OKAY TO PICK A LETTER TO SKIP (Q AND X CAN BE HARD TO LIST IN EVERY CATEGORY).

Purpose

A lot of teens struggle to imagine themselves as adults and even in a career they enjoy. Helping them develop a sense of purpose can be a huge image booster. Talk about the future with positive language and ask open-ended questions about what they look forward to about adulthood ("What do you imagine your life will be like five years from now?"). Talk about opportunities. Share your own past fears and share how you overcame them.

Introduce your teen to different career-oriented adults. Have conversations about the options based on their passions. Explore words like "job" versus "career." Talk about getting in on a career at the ground floor and working hard to achieve different levels of success.

Exposing your teen to different generations can help them wonder about their own future. When you have adult company, don't hesitate to include your teen in the conversation. Treating them like children will only perpetuate the idea that they don't have anything to contribute yet. Be intentional about having activities for teens and adults. Plan a game night, for example, where teens and adults can interact as peers. At Thanksgiving, get rid of the "kid table" and mix up the group. If you see them as young adults, they may start to get that vision for themselves.

True acceptance

Pick your battles. Let's say your teen wants to wear all black and have blue hair; ask yourself if this is the biggest issue. Be sure this is the fight you want to have. For some parents, it can be an important conversation; for others, it doesn't really matter. Not everything they do differently from you is worth arguing about. Often, they are going through phases. Give them time to decide about their choice. Listen to their reasons for trying something new and different.

They are going to make mistakes (didn't you? We both remember '80s hair…yikes). How do you separate out their awful behavior or choices from who they are as a person? Remember, bad behavior is often a symptom of their struggle or a broken system. Would you want to be defined by your mistakes (especially the ones you made when you were younger)? How do you show them they are lovable under everything?

Finding balance beyond what they look like means understanding and accepting who they are as a whole person. It means loving their strengths and having compassion for their weaknesses. Let their character be the focus for building your parent-teen relationship

Special Issues

Some families are dealing with very specific and very challenging situations. We are only going to touch on these subjects lightly here, but we recommend more research or reaching out to a professional if you are dealing with any of these topics.

Self-harm

Some teens participate in self-harm. Some parents will immediately think their teen is suicidal and panic. Take a deep breath. Suicidality is VERY different from self-harm. They are not often linked. When teens are doing things like cutting, they are sending a message and/or practicing control over their inner chaos. If they are sending a message, they want their inner pain to be seen by others on the outside. This kind of self-harm is often visible. It is a cry for help. If they are trying to control their pain, they will cut or harm themselves hoping to focus their inner turmoil. If their inner turmoil is that big, they need help. It could even be both.

Cutting and self-harm is the rawest way for a person to say, "Help!" The cutting causes a dopamine spike and helps the teen focus on the pain in one part of their body. It largely shows they have hope to make a change for themselves. They want to stop what is happening with their out-of-control emotions.

If you have a teen who is self-harming, you would be best served to see it as a big "I need someone to listen to me!" If, as a parent, you feel overwhelmed by their chaos, it may be time to connect with a professional mental health specialist who could be the adult in their life who listens. Family therapy can be a great way to develop communication skills together.

Eating disorders

There are three primary eating disorders that people suffer with: anorexia, bulimia, and binge eating. Each of these struggles impacts our teens with lifelong challenges if not recognized and treated early.

Each of these disorders stems out of a lack of self-esteem and sense of self. A teen's life can feel very chaotic, so regulating what they eat becomes a very strong coping skill for feeling "in control."

Some early warning signs parents should be aware of are:

- Obsessively comparing themselves to others
- Change in how they talk about food or their body
- Significant weight gain or loss
- New eating habits

The benefit of having a healthy and strong relationship with your teen will allow you to recognize early on any concerns your teen is struggling with and any changes they are demonstrating with eating or weight. Support your teen in making healthy choices about food. If possible, schedule a session with a nutritionist that you and your teen can attend together so that you are both learning and supporting each other with healthy eating. If you suspect your teen is suffering or beginning to suffer with an eating disorder, we highly advise finding a therapist who specializes in the treatment of eating disorders as soon as possible. The earlier the intervention, the better the odds are in overcoming this significant struggle.

How to talk about sex and our bodies

Every family has their way of talking about sex and their own personal moral compass. We are not here to tell you what that will look like. What we will encourage you to do, is start early talking to your kids about sex. By the time they get to middle school, they will start hearing things from their friends, online influencers (TikTok and YouTube), and, accidentally, links online. A twisted version of sex is available online and easily accessible.

Prepare your kids to think safely and critically about the topic. Share what the family values are and avoid shaming. If shame is introduced, they will be less likely to come to you when they have questions or they are exposed to something they don't understand. The closer your relationship to your teen is, the more they will stick to the family values. Having respect and communication in the family will increase the chance of your teen listening to what you have to say about sex.

THRIVE and Not Just a Body

Trust—Trust that if you work toward being physically fit, you will increase self-acceptance and improved mental health.

Heal—Healing is a process, so making the choice to nurture your body can start at any time.

Respect—Respect the whole person in your teen.

Invite—Invite your teen into a dialogue on eating right, exercising, and general health.

Validate—Validate their emotions of insecurity and struggles with body image while encouraging healthy goals.

Enjoy—Have some fun with activities that encourage physical movement.

Chapter 8

MORALS, VALUES, FAITH, AND SPIRITUALITY

We wanted a chapter on morals, values, faith, and spirituality because we both seem to encounter this topic often with the people we see in counseling. Both of us have somewhat different views on faith and will not be trying to convince you of any specific belief (we have our own private experiences, and you have yours). We are going to approach this chapter from a more general parenting perspective. Even if you don't have a specific faith you follow, this chapter could be important because we all have certain codes of ethics that we try to instill into our children. This is about raising responsible adults with strong character and integrity.

Know Yourself First

If you expect your teen to understand your values, it might be a good idea to know what you believe, especially if you are parenting with a partner or co-parenting. Having arguments with another caregiver about what you value will not strengthen anyone's point. It may even confuse your teen more. You may not agree, but it will be important to talk about your other caregiver's beliefs with respect and agree on what you want for your teen.

You may not need to have this conversation. You may be solid in your belief system and already know exactly what values are important to you. You may even know how to talk to your teen about religion, sex, drugs, dating, and going to parties. But if you don't, just know that not talking about it is rarely the answer. You should be prepared to have these conversations. If you don't, they will get the information from somewhere else.

Don't assume you will not have to have the conversation with *your* teen. Even if they are not behaving in a way that warrants deep conversations, they may have friends who are, and they may have questions. Are you going to be the parent they can talk to openly and honestly with? Will you be who they get solid answers from? Topics can sometimes be overwhelming for teens when they see their peers going through tough times.

Are you prepared if your teen comes to you with misinformation? How will you handle setting them back on track? Freaking out and yelling usually don't do the trick. Here's a tip from the therapy world; when you are faced with a bold statement that catches you off guard, just repeat it back word for word. For example, your teen says, "Someone told me our religion believes XYZ." You feel shocked inside and are stumped for words. Try saying something like, "Hmm. So you heard we believe XYZ? That's interesting. Let's talk about that. Can you give me more context about your conversation?" You just bought yourself some time to think.

Be careful if you talk about other teens because your teen is seeing it through the filter of how you see them. An off-hand remark about the neighbor's kid can easily be used to lower your own teen's self-esteem. Your values are modeled in how you treat others. Consider the following scenarios:

- Parent says: Did you see the neighbor's kid? He's getting fat.
    - Teen might think: Do my parents care a lot about the way I look? Do I need to be skinny for my parents to

approve of me? Maybe I should use laxatives like my friend. They swear it keeps the weight off.
- Parent says: That girl down the street is sleeping with her boyfriend. She's such a slut.
  - Teen might think: My partner pushed me farther than I was planning. I don't want to tell my parents because they will think I am a slut too.

Your teen is listening, and their filter is different than yours. They hear everything you say and will sometimes use it to judge themselves harshly. Even sarcasm can be ill-used. Use it sparingly. A healthy relationship with your teen is based on open communication and guidance.

TRY THIS
WHAT DO YOU BELIEVE?

THIS IS FOR THE PRIMARY CAREGIVER(S). ANSWER SOME BASIC QUESTIONS ABOUT YOUR FAITH TO HELP YOU HAVE AN OPEN CONVERSATION WITH YOUR TEEN. BEING PREPARED CAN HELP YOU STAY CALM AND RECEPTIVE TO QUESTIONS THEY MAY HAVE.

- WHY DO YOU BELIEVE WHAT YOU BELIEVE?
- HOW DID YOU COME TO THIS BELIEF OR VALUE SYSTEM?
- WHAT ARE THE BENEFITS OF YOUR VALUES?
- WHAT ARE THE CHALLENGES?
- WHAT FEELS LIKE THE "BLACK AND WHITE" RULES?
- WHAT ARE THE GRAY AREAS, AND HOW DO YOU FEEL ABOUT THOSE VALUES?
- ARE THERE ANY DIFFICULT TOPICS ABOUT WHICH YOU DON'T KNOW MUCH OR HAVE NOT DEVELOPED OPINIONS (SELF-HARM, SUICIDE, EATING DISORDERS, DEPRESSION, TEEN PREGNANCY)?

Values development

Values are personal, individualized, and not meant for judgment. Everyone has their own set of values based on their own belief system and experiences in life. The hope as parents is to instill our values into our children. Issues often arise when we say we value one thing, but our actions do not support our statement. So we are either mislabeling or losing touch with our value.

For example, a father states he values his family. When asked about what behaviors in the last week demonstrate this value, he states, "I worked sixty hours so they can have a nice lifestyle." His value of "family" was in question not because he doesn't love his family, but because his actions appear to value being a "provider." This is not a negative value to have, but it is important to identify the value correctly, sending a clear message to our teens about what our values are. Your teen might be thinking to themselves, *My dad cares more about money or working than he cares about me*. This is just the opposite message of what the father is trying to convey. The teen who may want a dad who values family might have the expectation that he would come home from work on time and do activities with his family members. The dad who values being a provider may think working long hours and putting in extra time will help the family have financial stability. Understanding both perspectives can be an opportunity to invite a dialogue sharing their mutual viewpoints.

Often adults can list off their top three values fairly quickly. But when we ask about the behaviors to support those values sometimes, they struggle. We tell our clients in therapy, "I should be able to follow you around for an entire week and be able to identify your values, not by what you tell people, but by what your actions show me."

There may be some values you have not fully developed in your own life. List the top three to five things you value in life (faith, success, respect, etc.) and take a close look at the week you just had and list how you have lived out that value for each one. For example:

1. Relationships—I called my friend to check up on them because we haven't talked in a while.

2. Family time: I missed all the family dinners because of work.
3. Hard work and providing for my family—I was on time and finished all my projects at work.

Some things you may find you gave focus to. Others you may have let slide. It's okay. This is not about shame and defending your week. This is about moving forward and living in your value system. Over the next few weeks, list what you accomplished in your top values. Make plans to take steps toward those values. This exercise sometimes causes people to shift their expectations or their actions. You may find your behavior is not aligned with what you wrote down as your top values.

A lot of people think they know what they value, but they are not actually living it out. Parents will have expectations of their teens to live out the parents' values (curfews, doing chores, time with family, etc.). If you aren't doing this, how do you expect your teen to? If you value respect but are yelling at your kids, how can you punish them when they yell back?

Adjusting your values to match your actions can sometimes take a little bit of honesty with yourself. Can you admit you may be acting on a different set of values than what you say were important? What does it mean? Do you need to adjust what you value or your actions? This is important. We have talked about how you should constantly be modeling the behavior you expect from your teen. If you say you value honesty but ask them to lie about their age to get a discount, what will they take away? In this example, maybe money is a higher value than honesty.

Passing on Your Belief System

Parents hope their teen will gladly embrace the beliefs they raised them in. Parents see their young children following their lead and mimicking them. This builds a hope this behavior will just carry over into the teen years and on to adulthood. It's going to be a bit messier. It's during the mess of the teen years that some parents panic and start a power struggle over beliefs, morals, etc. Let's try to avoid that.

The power struggle

I know my kid, you might be thinking. *I have seen them through hard times, I have been there since the beginning, and I know everything they have been through.* Or maybe you don't know your kid at all. Maybe you just blended a family, fostered a child, or adopted one. Regardless of how well you knew your kid growing up; it's difficult to really know who your "teen" is because THEY don't even know themselves yet. You may know the little kid who used to walk around your house, but they are transitioning into an adult.

It might feel like you are supposed to know who they are since you have watched them grow up, but maybe that's not a safe bet. We talked about the identity phase in earlier chapters. Remember they are trying to figure out who they are as an individual, separate from the family. Even they are not sure who they are (so don't take it personally). They are uncertain about their future and don't want to be told who they are. They want to discover it for themselves.

They are going through so many changes, and when you put them in a defined box, they will push back. They do not want to be defined by you. Have you ever liked when people make assumptions about you that don't fit? Remember, a lot of what they are feeling right now is discomfort, with who they are and who they will become, and they need to figure it out. Most teens feel like who they are doesn't fit, and it's important to give them room to consider what kind of person they are.

Assumptions based on who they were as a kid will be rejected, and they may feel insulted if they are not given the space to try it on as an individual. How dare you know me better than I know myself! They are changing constantly, and they want to be seen for the "new" them they are defining. This could become a power struggle, or it can be a beautiful process of watching your child become an adult (with a messy bit in the middle).

Guiding them and having a say can happen if you are building trust and growing the relationship as it changes. If a stranger or acquaintance asked you for a difficult favor, you would be hesitant to help. You might even flat out refuse. If your loved one came to you looking for help, you would be more likely to respond positively. You might even be willing to do something difficult if you care about them enough. This is how relationship works. The more you know someone, the more you trust them and want to hear what they have to say. Be open to getting to know them as they mature.

The best thing you can do to pass on your morals, values, faith, and spirituality is to develop a great relationship with your teen. The THRIVE model is very helpful because it is a balanced look at connecting with your teen. Building trust, healing from power struggles, modeling respect, inviting them into a conversation, validating their journey, and enjoying the growth process are all part of passing along your morals, values, faith, and spirituality.

Trust building sometimes means being honest about your own struggle with your faith or spiritual journey. It's okay to share your own ups and downs. Remember you did not develop your beliefs at birth and just accept that. You thought about your values and adjusted them as you got older. You may still be adjusting your journey. Being vulnerable about how you have struggled and accepting that your teen will also struggle will build trust.

Have authentic and transparent conversations. Sometimes parents believe if they reveal something flawed about their own growing up, they think they are giving their teen permission to do the same. Speak from your own mistakes and growth. Talk about the challenges and consequences of your own lapses in judgment as a teaching tool. It can also show them empathy.

If you have already had power struggles over this topic, it's not too late to repair the damage. They are old enough and logical enough (they really are) for you to stop and say, "Listen, I know I have been pushing you lately on this topic, and that's not fair to you. I am interested in what you are thinking about and want to listen." Be prepared for things that don't match your beliefs. If it feels like they are off track, take time to consider your response. Research what they are sharing with you before disagreeing with them. Don't let your fear of what they believe throw you off track and put you in a reactive mood. Really listen. Stay calm. Show compassion for their process.

Listening does not mean you agree with their choices. Taking the time to process will avoid those knee-jerk reactions like "What? You don't believe that! That's just stupid." Take the time to have a conversation and help them use critical thinking to really process their ideas. If they are sharing ideas that are drastically different than yours, chances are they got these ideas from someone they trust. To counter those ideas, they need to feel like they can have a safe conversation with you. Name calling, definitive statements, and telling them "what they actually believe" will not win them over.

Some parents fear their teens are being disrespectful when they start to question their morals, values, faith, and spirituality. The parent feels insulted when their teen wants to ask questions and poke holes in what the parent has spent time developing into a belief system. They are not trying to insult you. It's not about you at all. You, modeling respect, while they go through this process will connect you more deeply, and they will hopefully pick up on how to talk about this respectfully.

This might be one of the best times to be a positive role model. Listen to what they are saying. Consider why they might be believing this or that. Make sure they know you heard them before reacting. A respectful answer is often just summarizing and asking, "Did I get that right? What am I missing?" Asking questions can help them stop and think more logically and not just passionately. Don't get frustrated with their emotions.

Try This
Debate Swap

Pick a topic you and your teen seem to be having trouble connecting on (politics, religion, social issues, etc.). Challenge them to swap positions, and each of you debates the other's point of view (this is a classic debate skill). Remember, they will be listening to see if you really understand their point of view. Make an effort to do their side of the argument justice.

Invite your teen to participate in conversations. Work on critical thinking skills all the time and help them ask questions. Give them an opportunity to debate topics with you in a safe way (no yelling, listen carefully, and don't use personal attacks). Share your heart and journey without expectation, but with transparency and passion. There is power in inviting them into your own journey and struggle. It's also okay to admit you don't understand what they are thinking or feeling. Collaborate and develop ideas together.

Do this at any chance you get and do it early. When the big issues come up, it's harder to start making changes at that point. Make dinnertime a regular time to have open discourse. Be careful not to lecture but have back and forth dialogue. Ask a lot of questions. Share honestly and be prepared to be contradicted with dignity.

Validating doesn't mean you have to agree with them. It means you understand the process they are experiencing. Validating is, "I can see why you are asking that question. It seems like an important question. Let me think about it a little before I respond." Take all the time you need to research your response. They may catch you off guard. That's okay. Stay calm and say you will get back to them.

It can be a challenge to hear your teen question your faith. Validating their process means not showing anger or defensiveness, but rather being calm and confident in your own beliefs. Just because they are asking questions, it does not necessarily indicate what they believe. Remember they are in a time of exploring who they are.

In all these processes, it may be important to remember to laugh and enjoy the struggle. When you take yourself too seriously, you might be too rigid and not allow for open discussion. Laugh at your own misunderstandings. Be happy your teen is thinking for themselves. Delight in the process of them even considering what they believe. If they take your belief system and test it, pull it apart, stretch it, and then accept it, they will more likely stick with it in adulthood.

TRY THIS
THE QUESTION GAME

Are you paying attention? Try having an entire conversation using only questions. Often the best response to a difficult question from a teen can be another question. This is a fun way to play with that concept. Example:

Person A. What do you think of the political climate?
Person B. Do you really expect me to answer such a
      deep question?
Person A. Shouldn't everyone have an opinion?
Person B. Will you judge me based on my answer?
Person A. I wouldn't do that (oops…not a question)

The first person to answer without using a question loses. This can also be a great car game for road trips.

Faith-Based Shame and Guilt

As a parent your own faith may lead you to feelings of shame and guilt, and we would invite you to spend some time exploring this for yourself as well as for your teen. Shame and guilt seem to come out of a lot of misunderstood views on faith. From our perspective, shame and guilt are not meant to be used as punishment but rather feelings triggered by actions in which we need to explore and learn from. Holding on to shame and guilt leads to not only long-term depression but also often repeated behaviors reenforcing the feelings. Ask yourself this, does your faith want you to continue to suffer or learn from your actions and become a better version of yourself? Some young clients come into therapy with what looks like spiritual abuse. They are marinating in shame based on how they interpret or misinterpret their faith. This not only leads them further from their faith but may also cause trauma, anxiety, and depression. Often, they can't forgive themselves and may view themselves as unworthy and unlovable.

Recovering from mistakes

Everyone makes mistakes…even you. Some teens take a heavy-handed view of their faith and apply it to themselves. They mess up and worry they have disappointed their parents and God. They get stuck in the shame rather than the recovery, maybe spending days, months, even years feeling guilt and shame about something. Some can end up spiraling to very dark places. Numbing behavior (drugs, eating disorders, self-harm, etc.) can even become a problem.

A healthier approach to shame is to use it to make productive choices. When your teen messes up or they feel the wave of shame hit them, have them take a few minutes to sit with it. After a few minutes, it's time to be productive with what they are feeling. Help them ask themselves questions.

- What can I do to make this right?
- What have I learned about myself?

- How do I repair the damage I did?
- Can I live with the consequences of my choices?
- What kind of support do I need in this process?

Helping your teen to recover with grace is probably the best gift you can give them. The measure of a person is not in their errors, but in how they correct them. As you help your teen move forward, don't use their past against them at another time. Once they have made amends or restitution, they should not be mocked or ridiculed for their past blunders.

Parents may feel a need to correct their teen's mistakes for them. This can be a bad idea. Give them an opportunity to fix their own blunders so that they can be empowered through the process. If an email needs to be sent to a teacher asking about grades, have them do it. If they insulted a neighbor, don't go over and apologize for them; have them brainstorm ways they can make it right and then let them follow through on it. Learning to make restitution shouldn't be a shaming thing, but an opportunity to empower.

A huge benefit to letting them face the consequences of their actions is that they may learn a lot about their own emotional regulation and having compassion for other people's emotions. Here's an example: Your teen drives into the neighbor's trash cans and breaks them. You sit down with them and ask them how they can fix it. They say they already picked up the garbage that spilled, but they are worried because they broke the can itself. They decide to go next door and speak to the neighbor. Alone, they go over and explain. The neighbor gets angry. A well-balanced teen would then show empathy, instead of being defensive, "Sir, I can understand why you are angry. You have every right to be. I would like to pay for a new can." This story ends with the teen walking away without shame and feeling he made things right.

Discipline and faith

Many religious parents use their beliefs to guide them in the moral structure they expect their teen to live by. They hope that a simple "well, you know what God has to say about that" will get them to follow the rules. This may be true if your teen has fully embraced the tenets of your faith. But if you are still building their desire to be part of your faith system and share your beliefs, then you may need to not use faith in your discipline until they fully understand it.

If you hear yourself angrily saying things like, "*The Religious Text* says that you should not…" then your child might be developing strong shame based on faith. Make sure you are explaining the meaning of your religious text so they have buy-in to the rules their faith expects them to follow. A list of rules with no meaning will be just that, a list of rules. Some teens may even develop a negative reaction to their faith, if all they know is how they have disappointed God and broken the rules of their faith. Most religions have very high standards of living. Helping your teen understand the grace aspect of your faith will help them (most religions have the concept of grace, although it may be defined differently by each religion.)

Some people will use their religious texts as a discipline tool. They may say, "You have behaved badly. The consequence is I'm going to have you read or memorize this passage from our religious text." You have just made your religious text a punishment, rather than a joy to go to. You are welcome to keep doing that, but it will develop the idea in them that reading your religious text is a negative consequence. Saving memorization and reading of religious texts for family time can be a more positive interaction. Show them your joy in reading and memorizing, and they will feel that passion.

Try This
Family Book Club

This is a great summer activity. Pick a book (maybe one of the books from their school summer reading lists) and read it as a family. Either read it aloud, read it individually, or even get the audiobook and listen together. Plan a fancy dinner (in or out) and have a discussion about the book.

I (Stephanie) homeschooled, and we often had a book we read as a family. The dinners were fun and the conversations lively. Some of our favorites were *Lord of the Flies*, *Fahrenheit 451*, *Animal Farm*, and *To Kill a Mockingbird*.

This is a great activity to develop critical thinking and adult discussion. Encourage them to disagree with your point of view. Have them explain why they feel the way they do. Remember to use respectful language and make NO personal attacks when disagreeing (so no, "Well that's stupid").

Serving Others

One of the best ways to help anxiety and depression is to adjust one's focus. Therapists often get asked, "How can I get out of my head? I just keep ruminating on my troubles." Helping or serving others and directing one's thoughts on someone other than the self can be a powerful tool. Remember, at this age, your teen is focusing a lot on who they are, how they fit in, and if they are accepted. Sometimes they need a break from all the self-thought, and they may not even realize it.

Getting involved in volunteer work or a community project can be a huge self-esteem booster and a wonderful distraction from their thoughts. It may teach them empathy for people who live differently from them, pride in their neighborhood, compassion for people who are struggling, or just a sense of accomplishment.

The service can be big or small. It can be as simple as getting involved in a community trash pickup, helping with pet adoptions at a local store, spending time in a food bank, visiting elderly people, helping an ill neighbor do their shopping, etc. Brainstorm with your teen. Find out their passion and help them use it to serve. The skills they will develop in this kind of project can be life changing. Many schools demand their students do some community service to graduate. Don't minimize this. Help them find pleasure and joy in helping others.

Integrating Mindfulness with Your Faith

Mindfulness has become a very popular tool in the therapy world. It's basically about focusing on what is happening now and being extra present to your actions. It is also about taking responsibility in real time for one's choices. Some people hear mindfulness or meditation, and they think it's from some specific religion. It's not. Mindfulness goes way beyond just meditation. Surprisingly, almost every religion mentions meditation in some form or other, saying a rosary, praying, reading the bible, reading affirmations, walking in nature, etc. Almost all faiths call people to slow down and be present. That's what this is about.

It's about giving your full attention to all your activities and being the best version of yourself. Whether it's the disciplines of your faith, work, eating, sleeping, friendship development, etc., it's about being intentional. Taking responsibility for your life and making choices now that affect your future path.

It's easy to go through your day without being aware of the specifics of your tasks. How many times have you watched TV with a cell phone in your hand and realized at the end of a show you have no idea what happened? How many times have you scarfed down a meal and not even paid attention to the flavor? Think about all the aspects of your life that deserve your full attention. We live in a world of distractions.

It is often said anxiety is focusing on the future and depression is focusing on the past. Mindfulness brings us to what is happening now. It's about being in the present.

Anxiety and mindfulness

Mindfulness will help your teen to slow down. People with anxiety would do well to take some quiet time. Many religions encourage prayer, reading or listening to their texts, or listening to certain kinds of music. These things allow for relaxation and a connection to God. Even people who don't have a belief system can learn from this action of slowing down and breathing.

Two of the systems we have in our body are the sympathetic nervous system and the parasympathetic nervous system. The sympathetic nervous system is our active, fight-or-flight system. It controls the body's response to perceived threats, increases your heart rate, and pumps adrenaline into the body. It's where all the action happens. The parasympathetic system slows us down. It helps us rest. Our heart slows down, and we feel calmer (Latham, 2021).

Anxiety is our body hanging out in the sympathetic nervous system. Any person who has had an anxiety attack will tell you their heart was racing and they felt like they were in danger. The adrenaline might also cause them to struggle to get a good night's sleep. The fears come from worrying about the "what ifs…" of their future. Even when they are worrying about a past encounter (like a social situation), they are worried about future consequences "What did they think of me? Will they still want to be my friend?" They get focused on what horrible thing might happen, and they get stuck in the sympathetic system.

In mindfulness, you counter the "what ifs" by asking, "Can worrying now help this situation at all? Are there any what ifs that are positive that I have not considered?" Work with your teen to stop and breathe occasionally. Make a game of it. Often parents ask, "How was your day?" If you are getting the one-word response, try asking, "What went well today? What was a challenge today?" All teens should learn a few skills for calming any inner turmoil.

TRY THIS
SLOWING DOWN

Here are some practical ways to slow down you can easily teach your teen. You can even do these activities together:

- Meditate: Pick a word or sentence and repeat it while breathing slowly. Try breathing in through the nose on a count of seven, fill your belly like a balloon, and breathe out through the mouth on a count of eleven.
- Gratitude journal: Take a few minutes every day and think about three things to be grateful for that day. Even the smallest thing can be worthy of one's gratitude.
- Stare: Use either a candle, or an hourglass, or another form of moving visual (think of the lava lamps of the 1970s). Stare at the movement and count your deep breaths.
- Heartbeats: Using a digital watch with heart monitor. See if you can slow your heart rate using deep breaths.

Slowing down allows the body to go into rest mode and switch to the parasympathetic nervous system. These activities can be great for before bedtime or early morning, when most people have the worst anxiety.

Depression and mindfulness

Depression is often the teen feeling a lack of motivation and feeling sadness or disconnection from the world around them. It can often be triggered by an incident in the past that weighs on them. It can also be a chemical or hormonal imbalance, so it is always suggested they get a physical with their doctor when starting therapy.

Depression often means they are stuck in their parasympathetic nervous system.

It's amazing how many teens love scary movies. It's possible they are attempting to "jump start" their sympathetic nervous system and not even know it. When they feel lethargic and unmotivated, that boost of adrenaline is what they crave. With depression, meditation might not be the mindfulness activity of choice. The depressed teen is already slowed down. Teaching your teen intentional choices can be powerful. Engaging in physical activities with your teen is a great way of boosting their system.

With depression, your teen has an opportunity to be a person of integrity. Even when they say, "I don't really feel like doing it. I just don't feel motivated." Help them to choose one action; small or large, they can complete in that moment. Then teach them to push through that feeling and show integrity to their word. Talk about how much you appreciate their effort in trying, even when it's hard.

Mindfulness is about being intentional. It is choosing actions based on morals, values, faith, and spirituality.

THRIVE and Morals, Values, Faith, and Spirituality

Trust—Trust your teen's process of learning their own value system.

Heal—Mindfulness is a valuable mental health tool that can provide healing with depression and anxiety.

Respect—Respect that your teen may have a different spiritual journey than you.

Invite—Invite your teen into healthy dialogues about what you each believe

Validate—Validate their process and questions, by avoiding defensive responses and giving thoughtful answers.

Enjoy—Enjoy sharing your morals, values, faith, and spirituality with your teen by helping them experience the benefits of your belief system.

Chapter 9

HAVING FUN AND UNPLUGGING

It would be nice to say, "Have fun," and that's the end of the chapter, but there is some depth to this idea that may seem so simple on its surface. For some families, being intentional about having fun can make or break the whole idea of connecting with your teen. People can get wrapped up in the daily stressors so much that this becomes their only focus. Parents may become tempted to make every moment an exercise in helping their teen problem solve their stressor. What if not talking about it for a bit and having a little fun is the best option?

Ask yourself, is every interaction with your teen an exercise in discipline, a lecture on behavior, an effort to help "fix" them, or an argument? Can you imagine what it might be like for your teen to always hear about ways of how they could be doing better? They may start feeling defective and defeated.

Are you tired of being the parent who "nags" or seems angry most of the time? Do most of your interactions with your teen end the same way?

- "You always pick on me!"
- "I can't do anything right!"

- "Okay! I know!"
- The quiet seething stares

These reactions are telling you something. Is it possible your teen is not being intentionally rude, but sharing their internal belief they are getting everything wrong? Could they now be defining themselves by the problems they are struggling with (bad grades, anxiety, depression, lack of motivation, anger, etc.)? Could they be hurting and want to hurt you back, so they lash out? Just know that if you are not having fun with them, they are not having fun with you.

Guidelines to Planning Fun

Here are some guidelines to planning some fun activities and interactions. These are not strict rules, but just some ideas to consider. Not every family reacts to humor and fun the same way. Keep your family in mind. You know them better than anyone else. Fun should be just that—fun.

Choose something they like

Your idea of fun and your teen's idea of fun might be two very different things. You might think the event you are planning sounds terrific, but you may want to stop and assess who your teen is. Choosing the right activity is also telling your teen that you are taking into consideration what they like. Did you plan a hike for a teen who hates exercise? Did you take a kid with eating issues out for ice cream? Did you choose something loud and public for your quiet, indoor teen who may have social anxiety?

Taking time to understand your teen sends an important message that you accept them for who they are. When planning fun activities, don't assume that because they liked something five years ago, they will like it now.

You may have to do something you are not good at or spend time doing something you don't love. I (Stephanie) once spent an afternoon trying to learn my sons' Special Ops video game. I hate these kinds of games, but they loved it. They were laughing so hard. I could not figure out the controller buttons. I kept shooting the wrong thing and dying. It's been almost ten years since that afternoon, but they still joke about it and laugh.

Be ready to laugh at yourself

Doing something awkward may give you an opportunity to level the playing field if your teen struggles with self-confidence. Being able to laugh at yourself is a great way to break the ice with your teen. This is also an important skill to teach your teen. If you can't make fun of yourself, you may find they struggle with it too. They may be taking criticism and negative comments too seriously. This is a great way to model embarrassing and awkward moments.

One of the best lessons from trying new things as a family is making mistakes, laughing at yourself, and recovering. Show your teen how you can have grace when you don't do something perfectly. Show them it's okay to try something that might fail. So many teens struggle with perfectionism (parents too). Break this! Do something that will show your teen how to handle a struggle. Laugh.

TRY THIS
HIDE THE RAT (CLOWN, SPIDER, ETC.)

FIND SOMETHING SMALL AND WEIRD LIKE A STUFFED RAT, A CREEPY TOY CLOWN, A RUBBER SPIDER, ETC. THEN START HIDING IT FROM EACH OTHER. EVERY TIME A FAMILY MEMBER FINDS IT, IT IS NOW THEIR TURN TO HIDE IT FROM SOMEONE ELSE. BE CREATIVE. THE ITEM CAN BE HIDDEN IN GYM BAGS, LUNCH PAILS, OR UNDER PILLOWS—THE OPTIONS ARE ENDLESS. YOU CAN ALSO INCLUDE OTHER FRIENDS AND FAMILIES TO EXPAND THE FUN. MAYBE EVEN HAVE A CHAT GROUP TO REPORT THE MOST RECENT SURPRISE LOCATION.

Timing can be important

One thing that should be considered, as you show your teen respect, is scheduling around their plans. Your teen is old enough to have some control over their calendar. They may have planned schoolwork, an outing with a friend, a group event on a video game, etc. When you are planning something fun, the timing should not be something that creates an argument.

Pick a time that works for the whole family. Asking your teen when they are available, rather than demanding their time, shows them you are being considerate of their ability to make adultlike choices. Remember that teens are stuck between childhood and adulthood. Being asked if they are available shows them that you understand that they may have their own things planned.

Include others

Having other families your teen likes participate in your adventures can be a great way to have your teen participate with a better attitude. They may not feel happy with you lately, but they may have other people they enjoy spending time with. Include some of those people in your new adventures. This can be a great way to start to show your teen you are wanting to have fun with no other agenda.

Sometimes, the smartest thing to do is to include their best friends. You get to know them better, and that might give you better insight into your teen. They may sometimes feel like "an odd person out" when hanging out with the family. Having their best friend with them will give them support.

You may be doing these outings with your friends or even (if a single parent) a partner who is new to the family. Be sure not to get caught up in putting all your attention into your friends. These events are about connecting to your teen and having fun. Your mantra might be "It's not about me. I'm connecting with my teen." If they seem quiet or uncomfortable, try to pay attention to them. Don't get distracted by your own needs. Keep in mind the goal of building relationship with your teen.

Expectations

Make sure your expectations aren't ruining your time. If you set your hopes too high early on, then you may feel resentment that your teen isn't excited about whatever you have planned. They may not show appreciation. Look for the more subtle connections that they are enjoying their time with you. Them laughing with you can be a great sign that they are appreciating your plans. Even a lack of complaining can be a good sign. Be patient. This takes time.

Expectations for fun time need to be made clear with the family ahead of time. If you have rules around things like cell phone use or participation, let everyone know. If there are other adults in the group, get buy-in from them on the expectations before communicating it to your teen. Another adult in the group acting disrespectfully toward you and your rules can be very divisive.

Try to have the same rules for the teens in the group as for the adults (you want to move more and more toward treating them like adults in most situations). If cell phones are expected to be put away, then put yours away as well. Don't ask for them to participate in your activity if you aren't willing to participate in things they might suggest.

Be confident in your choices

If you plan well, be confident in your plan. If your family members seem hesitant, be encouraging and show them you know what you are doing. Sometimes a teen will take advantage of uncertainty; don't let them shut down your plans with negative comments. If you expect them to be hesitant, then it will be easier to validate their reluctance with a relaxed tone.

Challenge them to think differently. It's okay to admit, "I know our family has been at odds lately, and I'm trying to change that. I want us all to do something fun together. I have a great plan…" You are not trying to trick them, so it doesn't need to be a secret. You can talk to your teen about how you feel your family is long overdue for a fun activity.

Instead of asking IF they want to join you, ask them WHEN. This way you are showing confidence. While you are out, remind them they can do the activity with either a positive attitude or a negative attitude. Then let them be how they want to be. We know that hanging out with a brooding teen can be a real downer but give it time. Often their sulky mood improves if you don't pay it a lot of attention.

Understanding moods

One thing to keep in the back of your mind is that if your teen has a problem with depression, they may struggle to be excited about anything. Don't take it personally. Some teens are very shy or introverted and struggle to be talkative. That doesn't mean they aren't participating. Sometimes choosing a calmer activity is keeping your teen in mind.

Being aware of your teen's moods will help you have more realistic expectations. Telling them to smile and to have a better attitude will just feel like more criticism. In the story of Winnie-the-Pooh, they still included Eeyore even though he was sullen all the time (Milne, 1926). Let your teen feel accepted as they are. Remember that this is NOT the time to be "fixing" your teen and their issues.

Suggestions

SINCE COVID-19, MANY WEBSITES OFFER CLASSES IN ALL KINDS OF AREAS, FROM COOKING TO DANCING. SIGN UP AS A FAMILY. LET YOUR TEEN PICK THE TOPIC. YOU CAN ALSO FIND VIDEOS FOR FREE THAT TEACH ALL KINDS OF THINGS. SOME SUGGESTIONS MIGHT BE:

- Learn something new together (instrument, cooking, art, sport, game, etc.)
- Do something spontaneous and simple
  - Suggest miniature golf after dinner on a Wednesday
  - Do a blackout night, turn off the lights, get candles, play games, hide-and-seek

- o   Go to the drive-in with lots of snacks
- Play a cooperative board game (Hanabi, Dead of Winter, Legends of Andor, Time Stories, etc.; search the Internet for great suggestions. Some libraries have games available to play for the budget conscious)
- Create a random goal to accomplish as a family
  - o   Find the perfect burger/pizza
  - o   Climb the tallest local peak
  - o   Push-up challenge
  - o   Plan a $5 dinner for the whole family
- Create a funny video as a family
- Try an "escape room" or do a mystery in a box (examples: Hunt a Killer Mystery, Unsolved Case Files).
- Be tourists in your own town by looking up touristy activities to do
- Ropes course, whitewater rafting, or other outdoor team building activity

Consequences with Compassion

An aspect of fun that most people don't think about is using humor in your discipline. It is not always appropriate, but sometimes it's perfectly warranted. If you are creating boundaries around tech, attitude, and chores, you can create some strange consequences that also affect the adults in the house. Example: Imagine that anyone who uses their cell phone at the table must wear a large, weird hat for the rest of the meal. Now imagine Dad has used his phone and the whole family laughs together as he wears "the hat." Remember that if your teen is not laughing with you, you may be mocking them in their discomfort, in which case change your plan.

Too many people think "punishment" needs to be angry and painful. You are not trying to hurt your teen or create pain; you are trying to teach them. Give them a creative consequence that will help them remember to change their attitude.

You don't need to be visibly "angry" (yelling, rejecting, etc.) to convey you are upset about their behavior. It's okay to have a calm, loving attitude toward your teen, even when handing out consequences. You can even convey a feeling of empathy, "I know you really wanted to go to that event. You also know there must be consequences for your behavior. If you want, we can watch a movie together." They may not take you up on it because they may be angry, but you don't need to be upset.

When the world serves up natural consequences for your teen, you don't need to add to it. For example, if they get a speeding ticket, the cost will be painful enough (if they don't have the money, make them earn it). You don't need to add to their punishment by yelling or lecturing them.

I (Stephanie) heard a story about a mom whose teen came home drunk. The mom set up a recording device and sat down for a conversation. She asked him all kinds of informative questions. The next morning at breakfast, the mom played back the conversation to her son. He was mortified by the things he said. He never came home drunk again.

Being creative may not always work. Even a classic structure of consequences can go upside down at times. Keep trying and stay consistent with your expectations. Be sure to clearly state consequences to your teen.

TRY THIS
DINNER CONSEQUENCES

This is an exercise that can be done with everyone in the family. At dinner, create a list of behavior that need to be improved. Allow your teen to add to the list so they can also include Mom and Dad's behavior in the process. The list should include frustrating behavior:

- Eating with your mouth open
- Forgetting to say, "Please," when asking someone to pass something
- Cell phone use

Everyone starts the dinner with five to ten tokens. As the meal progresses, people can be caught breaking the rules and must pay a token to the middle of the table. The person with the least number of tokens does the dishes. If it's a tie for least number of tokens, then those people work together to clean up after dinner.

Unplugging

We can't emphasize enough how important unplugging can be. Technology and digital health are impacting our families in many ways, and the electronic connection is a way of life today. We use our electronic gadgets to work, go to school, socialize, etc. They are in our houses, cars, schools, everywhere. We could spend an entire chapter discussing the pros and cons of digital health on our teens, adults, and families, but we really just want to take a moment to emphasize the importance of actual human, uninterrupted interactions.

Keep in mind, many parents have a cell phone in their hand most of the time. Are you such a parent? If that describes you, it may be time to model unplugging. The reality of today's world is that it is almost impossible to get stuff done without the Internet or a smartphone. That doesn't mean we can't take time off from our technology and screens.

Like parent, like teen

We've talked a lot about how modeling different behavior will help teach your teen. It may mean you need to be honest with yourself about your tech consumption. Do you talk to people with a phone in your hand? Do you have a screen on when you are eating a meal? Do you use the Internet for time-wasting activities? Do you interrupt important family time to answer your cell or respond to a notification? If so, we are encouraging you to challenge yourself and your entire family with the idea of unplugging.

Tech and screens are not evil. They are useful for a lot of things. But learning tech boundaries and modeling them are a great way to teach boundaries in general. Maybe it's as simple as having a "cell-phone-free zone" in the kitchen or a time of day that is "tech-free." Just remember to follow your own rules. We highly recommend that a basket be placed in your dining area, and every time someone goes to the table for a meal, they turn off their ringers, place the electronic device in the basket, and then join each other at the table. Use this time for interactions, good conversations, and a quiet moment of focus.

Expect withdrawals

When people are truly hooked on something like technology, then you can expect some withdrawal symptoms when they are pushed to give it up. Excuses and lying about behavior are normal when dealing with an addiction. Someone who is honest and kind will hide things and lie when they are addicted to it. When you finally do get your teen away from their screens, you can expect sadness, anxiety, sleeplessness, and irritability.

The detox period can be difficult. Not only be firm in your boundaries, but also have compassion for their experience. It is okay to let them know, "You are acting disrespectfully. Please take some downtime in your room." They may try to debate or push for a change, in an effort to get their tech back; stay strong and remember this is a temporary transition.

Be savvy

Know their favorite YouTube Channels. Who are they following on TikTok? Many teens will create secret accounts to hide from their parents. If you have "parent" controls, they often find ways around it. We would also suggest a basic phone instead of a smartphone. Many of the tech giants, like Steve Jobs and the likes, didn't let their own kids use their own technology. "Research has found that an eighth-grader's risk for depression jumps 27% when he or she frequently uses social media" (Akhtar & Ward, 2020).

Understanding what they are capable of and what they are consuming online will provide safety. They can easily be led down Internet "rabbit holes" that may bring harm to your teen or family. It is your responsibility to provide a safe structure for them online.

Boredom

Boredom is a skill not an affliction. Children often come to their parents whining, "I'm booooored." Many modern parents think they need to solve this problem. They offer solutions and ideas, only to have their child say, "Nooo." Now they are teens and are probably still whining about being bored because they never learned how to entertain themselves. What if the solution is to let them be bored?

Boredom is the seed of innovation and creativity. When you take technology away, your teen is going to experience boredom possibly for the first time. Give them time to solve this on their own. "I bet you are bored. What a great opportunity to come up with something creative to do. Unless you want to help me clean and do laundry?" They will not usually be THAT bored. Now let it go and see what they come up with.

TRY THIS
DANCE MOVES

PICK A SONG FROM WHEN YOU WERE THEIR AGE AND TEACH THEM SOME OF YOUR TEEN DANCE MOVES (WHAT WERE THE TRENDS?). THEN GIVE THEM A CHANCE TO PLAY A SONG FOR YOU AND TEACH YOU SOME OF THEIR MOVES. BE PREPARED TO BE LAUGHED AT AND REMEMBER TO LAUGH WITH THEM.

Important Warning!

Your teen is not going to suddenly change into the I-love-hanging-out-with-you teen just because you read a book. Don't expect your teen to be on the same page...yet. Change takes time. You may offer up a fun evening, and they may scoff at you. The more you learn about being an active and thriving parent, you will want to give your teen time to catch up.

There has been a balance for a long time, and now it may be changing. They are not used to the "new way" and may fight it. As you make healthier options, you may find yourself facing opposition. Staying strong and consistent shows them that the "new way" is permanent and they can trust it. Keep creating fun moments so it doesn't all feel like work. They will eventually adapt.

This can be very daunting. You make a change and hope to get an encouraging response, and instead you get eye rolls, mocking, or rejection. This is where grit and tenacity will be your friend. The balance was broken, but it was familiar; most people hate change, even when it is healthy. Just because you are offering fun, it doesn't mean they will immediately accept the "new way." They will have doubts and may even struggle to trust anything you offer up. Stay calm. Make fun plans anyway. Make sure you are keeping their likes in mind. This is a journey, not a single event.

THRIVE and Having Fun

Trust—Build trust by being honest and consistent, even when you are having fun.

Heal—Be okay laughing together and even at yourself. Creating memories outside of all the chaos can be very healing.

Respect—Make sure rules and outings keep everyone in mind and respect each individual in the family.

Invite—Invite your teen to come spend time. Be sure to keep their schedule in mind. Include their friends if it means it will be a better event for everyone.

Validate—Validate your teen's unique personality by being aware of something they might not think is fun.

Enjoy—Have fun! Enjoy your family. Enjoy your teen.

Chapter 10

LIVING AND THRIVING

Trust—When you trust another person, you experience a feeling of safety. After years of parenting your teen consistently, with open communication and role modeling, you are creating a relationship based on mutual trust. Living in this type of environment allows you, the parent, to feel assured your teen can explore, grow, and experience life with all the confidence they have built up from trusting in your guidance.

Heal—Healing begins and ends with vulnerability. Having the humility to identify areas in your own life that need improvement allows your teen to do the same. Living in an environment where failure is recognized as a natural part of growth, your teen will be empowered to live more boldly knowing you have given them the skills to heal.

Respect—Mutual respect creates a long-lasting connection where individual ideas and opinions can be shared. Living in this type of relationship encourages critical thinking, honest discussions, and collaborative dialogue. Raising your teen with respectful communication may give them the desire to connect well beyond the teen years.

Invite—Inviting your teen into a collaboration with you builds their self-esteem and strengthens their feelings of acceptance. Living in a household where members participate and provide input affords practice in problem solving. Your teen will feel more confident as an adult, knowing you have invited them into this shared process.

Validate—Validation provides a sense of being heard. Living with this kind of support helps your teen regulate emotions and manage their thoughts. Even though you may not have agreed with all their choices, honoring their feelings and process will teach them to value themselves and others.

Enjoy—Have fun! Enjoy your family. Enjoy your teen.

QUESTIONS FOR *TABLE TALK*

1. If you could rewrite one moment in the last week, what would it be?
2. If you could change one rule at your school or work, what would you change?
3. If you could take a vacation with a friend (no family), who would you take, and where would you go?
4. What three characters in movies, TV, and books best describe you?
5. If you could live in your favorite book or movie, where would you live?
6. If you could go on a date with a character from a movie, TV, or book, who would you choose?
7. Describe a meal that makes you happy.
8. What meal can you make to impress your friends (if you don't have one—maybe design a menu you can learn to make together)?
9. What two songs best describe you?
10. If you felt sad, what song would you listen to? (Share it now.)
11. If you felt angry, what song would you listen to? (Share it now.)

12. If you feel like celebrating, what song would you listen to? (Share it now.)
13. Define success.
14. What does failure mean to you? Give an example in your life and what you did about it.
15. If you could talk to someone your age from one hundred years ago, what would you ask them?
16. If you could talk to someone a hundred years in the future, what would you want to know?
17. If you could switch places with someone you know, who would you switch with?
18. What is something you have created that you are proud of?
19. If you were a famous photographer, what story would your photography tell?
20. If you could own any animal in the world (without danger). what would you own?
21. Name two to three couples who are a great example of a good marriage.
22. What is your favorite joke?
23. What skill do you wish you could just know without having to learn it?
24. What childhood memory makes you sad and happy at the same time?
25. What was something silly you did as a kid you would never do now?
26. What is something you miss about being little?
27. You as a parent: What will be the same or different from your own parents?
28. What movie do you love that most people hate, or what movie do you hate that most love?
29. What would you buy with $10,000 if it had to be frivolous and you can't keep it?
30. If you could help one underserved population, who would you help?
31. What do you most want to be remembered for?

32. How do you feel about lying? Has it made your life easier or harder?
33. If you (and only you) had twenty-four hours to live, how would you spend that time?
34. If the world was going to end in twenty-four hours, what would you spend that time doing?
35. What do you wish the generation before you could understand better about your age group?
36. If money didn't matter, what job would you want to do right now?
37. What famous person could play you in a movie?
38. Who do you wish you could see again whom you haven't seen in a while?
39. Name a person you feel like you need to apologize to.
40. Describe three things you think will be very different in your life in five years.
41. If you had to be on a survival team with one person you know, who would you choose?
42. If you could be famous for something you already know how to do, what would it be?
43. What is the difference between a job and a career to you? Which is more important?
44. What do people get wrong about you?
45. Looking back, what do you wish everyone would forget happened?
46. If you got stuck on the same day for a month, what day would you choose?
47. If the whole world was listening to you right now, what would you say?
48. In what area of your life do you wish you were a little braver?
49. If you knew there would be a positive outcome, what is one thing you would do that seems too risky right now?
50. Challenge: Call someone you know and let them know you care about them.

Bibliography

American Psychiatric Association. "Diagnostic and statistical manual of mental disorders." Washington DC, 2022.

Berger, K. S. *The Developing Person through the Life Span.* New York: Worth, 2008.

Charles, R. "How introvert and extrovert brains differ: 6 differences according to science." Retrieved Aug 23, 2022, from Mind Journal: https://themindsjournal.com/honest-confessions-of-an-introvert/, n.d.

Digitale, E. "The teen brain tunes in less to Mom's voice, more to unfamiliar voices, study finds." Retrieved from Stanford Medicine: https://med.stanford.edu/news/all-news/2022/04/teenager-brain-mother-voice.html, 2022, April 28.

Dweck, C. *Mindset.* New York: Ballantine Books, 2006.

End Slavery Now. *Zach Hunter: Modern Day Abolitionist.* Retrieved from *End Slavery Now*: https://www.endslaverynow.org/blog/articles/zach-hunter-loose-change-to-loosen-chains, 2014, April 10.

Erikson, E. H. *Childhood and Society.* In E. H. Erikson. *Childhood and Society* (p. p262). New York: Norton, 1963.

Gillespie Shields Blog. "40 Facts About Two Parent Families." Retrieved from Gillespie Shields: Goldfarb & Taylor: https://gillespieshields.com/40-facts-two-parent-families/, 2016, October 3.

Hitchcock, A., Director. *Psycho.* Motion Picture, 1960.

Hughes, J., Director. *Breakfast Club.* Motion Picture, 1985.

Johns Hopkins Medicine. "Teenagers and Sleep: How Much Sleep Is Enough?" Retrieved November 2, 2021, from Johns Hopkins Medicine: https://www.hopkinsmedicine.org/health/wellness-

and-prevention/teenagers-and-sleep-how-much-sleep-is-enough, 2021.

Kardaras, N. *Tech Addiction and Digital Health in Children, Adolescents and Young Adults.* Pesi, 2020

Latham, K. "Sympathetic vs. Parasympathetic Nervous System." Retrieved from *Biology Dictionary.* https://biologydictionary.net/sympathetic-vs-parasympathetic-nervous-system/, 2021, February 20.

Milne, A. *Winnie-the-Pooh.* New York, 1926.

Nolan, C., Director. *Dark Knight.* Motion Picture, 2008.

Oelze, P. "There Are 6 Different Family Types And Each One Has A Unique Family Dynamic." Retrieved from *Better Help.* https://www.betterhelp.com/advice/family/there-are-6-different-family-types-and-each-one-has-a-unique-family-dynamic/, 2020, December 31.

Pickhardt, C. "Adolescence and Self-Esteem." Retrieved from *Psychology Today.* https://www.psychologytoday.com/us/blog/surviving-your-childs-adolescence/201009/adolescence-and-self-esteem, 2010, September 6.

Roberts, G. "Wheel of emotional words, in case you're having trouble finding the words these days." Retrieved from *FlowingData.* https://flowingdata.com/2020/03/20/wheel-of-emotional-words/, 2020, March 20.

Sedgwick, R. Epstein, S. Dutta, R. and Ougrin, D. "Social media, internet use and suicide attempts in adolescents." Retrieved from *Current Opinion in Psychiatry.* https://journals.lww.com/co-psychiatry/fulltext/2019/11000/social_media,_internet_use_and_suicide_attempts_in.12.aspx, 2019, November.

Skynner, R. "Robin Skynner > Quotes." Retrieved September 1, 2022, from Goodreads: https://www.goodreads.com/author/quotes/3133154.Robin_Skynner. n.d.

Stanford Children's Health. "Understanding the Teen Brain." Retrieved from *Stanford Children's Health.* https://www.stanfordchildrens.org/en/topic/default?id=understanding-the-teen-brain-1-3051, 2022.

TMI. "Teen Missions International." Retrieved from https://teenmissions.org/. 2022.

Waters, M., Director. *Mean Girls*. Motion Picture, 2004.

WebMD. "What Is Snowplow Parenting?" Retrieved from WebMD. https://www.webmd.com/parenting/what-is-snowplow-parenting#1, 2021.

Whyte, A. "The Connection Between Parenting Style and Bullying." Retrieved from Evolve Treatment Centers. https://evolvetreatment.com/blog/parenting-style-bullying/. 2021.

Wilson, G. *Your Brain on Porn: Internet Pornography and the Emerging Science of Addiction*. Greenwood. MS: Commonwealth Publishing. 2017.

About the Authors

Stephanie Iles is a Licensed Marriage and Family Therapist working in private practice. She graduated with a master's in marriage and family therapy from Western Seminary. She has spent two decades working with teens and families through youth ministry and her work as a therapist. Twelve of those years were spent working at her church in student ministries, mentoring teens. As a therapist, she worked for five years in a rural school with students heavily affected by gang culture. She also spent some time in private practice, working with families, couples, and individuals of all ages. She has experience working with families from different cultures and faiths, socioeconomic backgrounds, and people from the LGBTQ community. She raised and homeschooled her two boys, who are now successful adults, and she loves spending time with her grandkids. Currently she is living in a rural community with her husband and continues to work in private practice.

Angelé Suarez is a Licensed Clinical Social Worker who received her master's degree in social work from Colorado State University. With over twenty-two years of experience, Angelé has worked with adolescents and families, addressing challenges including family dynamics, trauma, and reunification. She has worked in a variety of clinical and leadership roles, such as a therapist, professor, consultant, and business owner. With each role, she has gained a better understanding of the value of meeting people where they are on their individual, family, and community life paths. Angele views her therapeutic role as an honor and privilege to support individuals, families, and communities. Currently, her greatest role is being a stepmother of four and living each day to appreciate and value our relationships.

www.ingramcontent.com/pod-product-compliance
Lightning Source LLC
Chambersburg PA
CBHW021209130726
47988CB00002B/576